Field Guide to
New Hampshire Trout Ponds

Field Guide
to New Hampshire
Trout Ponds

Paul VanderWende

BONDCLIFF BOOKS

LITTLETON, NEW HAMPSHIRE

Photos on pages 76 (*top*), 77 (*top and bottom*) and 110 (*top*)
by Steven D. Smith. All other photos by the author.

Maps courtesy of the New Hampshire Department
of Environmental Services.

Text composition by Passumpsic Publishing, St. Johnsbury, Vt.
Printed in the United States by Sherwin Dodge Printers, Littleton, N.H.

Additional copies of this book may be obtained directly from:
    Bondcliff Books
    P.O. Box 385
    Littleton, NH 03561

*This book is dedicated
to my wife Sarah.*

What a catch!

Contents

Carroll County

Sullivan and Cheshire Counties

Merrimack and Hillsborough Counties

Belknap, Strafford, and Rockingham Counties

Acknowledgments

I would like to thank the folks at the New Hampshire Fish and Game Department for their help and guidance on this project. I would also like to thank the New Hampshire Department of Environmental Services for their assistance with the lake and pond information. Inspiration for this book came in part from Gary Clark and his book, *Atlas of New Hampshire Bass Ponds*. I've used it countless times and found it extremely useful when looking for some place new and different to fish. Some of the distances in the lake descriptions were borrowed from him also. Special thanks go to Steve Smith, author of *Ponds and Lakes of the White Mountains*, for his input and suggestions on how to put a book together. I want to thank Bob Donnelly and Don Schrock for sharing their experiences fishing most of these ponds. Thanks to David Bateman for his help in clocking mileage and helping with the directions to a lot of these ponds. My deepest appreciation goes to my editor, publisher and friend Mike Dickerman for his patience and encouragement.

Introduction

Today's hectic world puts an increasing strain on the amount of personal time we have to pursue the more important things in life; i.e., fishing and boating. It's the time we spend on these recreational pursuits that we value more and yet seem to get lost in the pinch between work and other responsibilities. Whether you are fishing or just out to view nature on the water, it is the intent of this book to help you make better decisions on where and how to spend that valued time on the water. Hopefully this book will help you better prepare before heading out for the day by answering the basic questions such as: How do I get there? What is the ramp like? Will I be able to park? How deep is the lake or pond? What kinds of fish are there in it? Are there speed limits or motor restrictions?

For the most part, the bodies of water featured in this book are ponds or lakes easily accessible by motor vehicle. By no means are all of New Hampshire's trout ponds included; instead, we have tried to offer up a large sampling of some of the Granite State's better trout fishing ponds. A great resource for helping you get to the ponds is the *New Hampshire Atlas & Gazetteer* published by DeLorme and available in bookstores and sporting good stores across the region. Between the directions given in this book and the maps found in the *New Hampshire Atlas & Gazetteer* you shouldn't have any problem getting to any of the trout ponds featured on the following pages.

Now, here are a few words about:

The Information Pages

The lake and pond information is broken up into nine categories. Most are self-explanatory. In this book, the term "Clarity" refers to the depth at which a "Secchi Disk" is no longer visible. A Secchi Disk is a round disk divided into four equal sections painted in alternating black and white. The disk is lowered into the water on a rope or chain and the depth at which it is no longer visible is recorded.

The Depth Maps

The depth maps shown for each pond or lake in this book were provided by the New Hampshire Department of Environmental Services. The maps shown are meant to depict the general characteristics of the lake bottom and should not be relied upon for navigation.

Foreign Species

Non-native mussels and plants have wreaked havoc with many of the nation's waterways. In New Hampshire, "before you boat know what you tote." Exotic weeds have already been found in several of our lakes. Please be sure to clear all vegetation from your boat, kayak, canoe, and trailer before launching. If you have been in waters known to contain the zebra mussel please clean your craft thoroughly.

Fishing Rules and Definitions

Please refer to the current edition of the *New Hampshire Fishing Digest* (published by the N.H. Fish and Game Department) for up-to-date rules, regulations and licensing information. At the time of this printing, the digest defines the following terms:

Fly Fishing Only: "Fishing by trolling or casting with only fly rod, fly reel, and fly line combination with an artificial fly attached, and does not include the use of spinning, spincast, and casting rods and reels or lead core lines."

Rules for Lake Trout and/or Salmon Lakes:

"Minimum Length: Brook, Rainbow and Brown Trout and their hybrids, 15 inches; Lake Trout, 18 inches; Landlocked Salmon, 15 inches. The combined daily limit for Lake Trout, Salmon, Book Trout, Rainbow Trout, Brown Trout and their hybrids is two (2) fish."

The Lead Ban, Getting the Lead Out

In the *New Hampshire Freshwater Fishing Guide*, it is noted that "State law prohibits the use of lead sinkers and jigs in freshwater lakes and ponds in New Hampshire. The ban prohibits the use of lead sinkers weighing 1 ounce or less and lead jigs less than 1 inch long along their longest axis."

"Biologists have studied the effects of lead sinkers and jigs on water birds, such as loons and swans, since the 1970s. Their ongoing research has documented that in the Northeast United States and Canada where loons breed, lead sinkers or jigs can account for 10 to 50 percent of dead adult loons found by researchers."

I hope this book helps you find that New Hampshire's true wealth lies in the beauty found on its cold, clear lakes and ponds.

Good luck and good fishin'.

P.V.W.

Coös County

Fish Pond in Columbia

Akers Pond

ACRES: 309

MAX DEPTH: 26'   **MEAN DEPTH:** 10'

CLARITY: 11'   **ELEVATION:** 1231'

FISH SPECIES: Rainbow Trout, Largemouth Bass

ACCESS: A gravel ramp with good turnaround space and parking for 8–10 vehicles.

DIRECTIONS: From the intersection of Routes 16 and 26 in Errol, take Route 26 west 1.4 mi. to Akers Pond Road on the right. Continue 0.25 mi. to the launch on the right.

COMMENTS: A good, sizable pond with minimal development on its shoreline.

You can make an inexpensive rod holder from a 3- or 4-inch piece of PVC pipe. Glue one end cap on and leave the other removable. This will save a tremendous amount of wear and tear on your rods riding around all summer in a trunk or behind a truck seat.

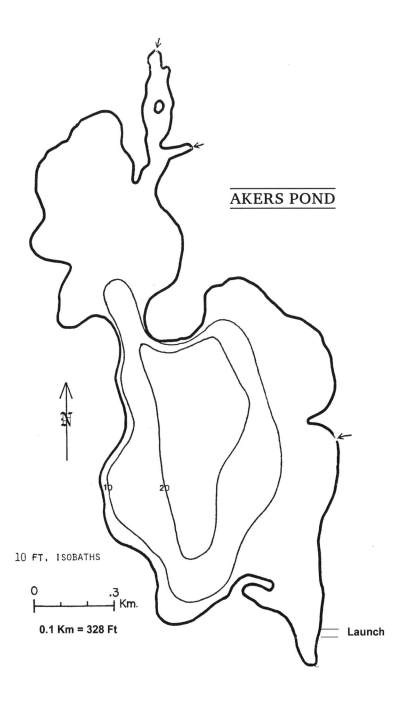

AKERS POND

N

10 FT. ISOBATHS

0 ———————— .3
|—————————————| Km.

0.1 Km = 328 Ft

⸺ Launch

Back Lake

ACRES: 359

MAX DEPTH: 15'   **MEAN DEPTH:** 7'

CLARITY: 8'   **ELEVATION:** 1575'

FISH SPECIES: Brook Trout, Rainbow Trout, Brown Trout, Horned Pout

ACCESS: A gravel ramp with parking for 8–10 vehicles. It also has a good turnaround

DIRECTIONS: A little north of Lake Francis, turn left off Route 3 and onto Spooner Road. This road follows along the southeast shore of Back Lake. Go 0.3 mi. to the launch on the right.

COMMENTS: This is typically a very good pond for fishing, although it can be pretty busy during the peak summer season.

> *Make sure your reel is filled with the proper amount of line. A correctly filled fishing reel will cast farther and reel faster.*

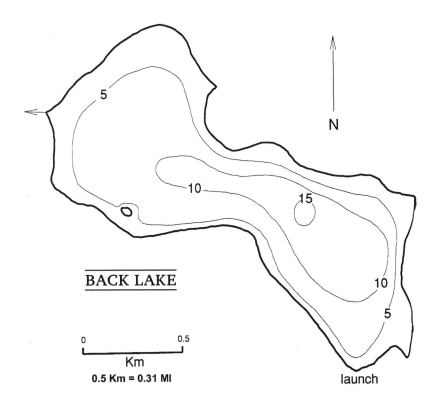

5

10

15

0

10

5

N

BACK LAKE

0   0.5
Km
0.5 Km = 0.31 MI

launch

Cedar Pond

ACRES: 78

MAX DEPTH: 56'   **MEAN DEPTH:** 31'

CLARITY: 12'   **ELEVATION:** 1113'

FISH SPECIES: Rainbow Trout, Smallmouth Bass, Pickerel, Horned Pout

ACCESS: A paved ramp with parking for 8–10 vehicles.

DIRECTIONS: From the intersection of Routes 110 and 110A in West Milan, take Route 110A east 1.8 mi. to the access area on the right across from a campground.

COMMENTS: Cedar Pond can get quite busy during the summer months and has heavy shoreline development. It is stocked with Rainbow Trout.

Before assembling a two-piece rod, rub the male ferrule through your hair. This will leave enough oil to make it easier to take apart later.

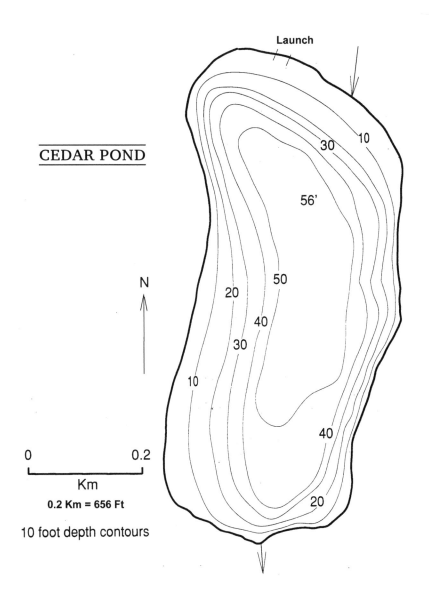

CEDAR POND

Launch

30   10

56'

50

N

20

40

30

10

0   0.2
Km
0.2 Km = 656 Ft

40

10 foot depth contours

20

Christine Lake

ACRES: 170

MAX DEPTH: 57'   **MEAN DEPTH:** 23'

CLARITY: 16'   **ELEVATION:** 1202'

FISH SPECIES: Brook Trout, Brown Trout, Smallmouth Bass

ACCESS: The launch is next to the town beach. There is parking for two trailers, but the turn-around is tight.

DIRECTIONS: From Route 110 in Stark, drive through the covered bridge and then bear right. Go 2.2 mi. to a fork and steer left (north). Go 0.3 mi. further to another fork and bear left again. The access is straight ahead.

COMMENTS: A nice scenic pond good for fishing *and* wildlife viewing. It is stocked with Brook Trout. There is a 10-horsepower limit on motors for all boats on Christine Lake.

> *One very important piece of fishing equipment:*
> *a spare set of car keys!*

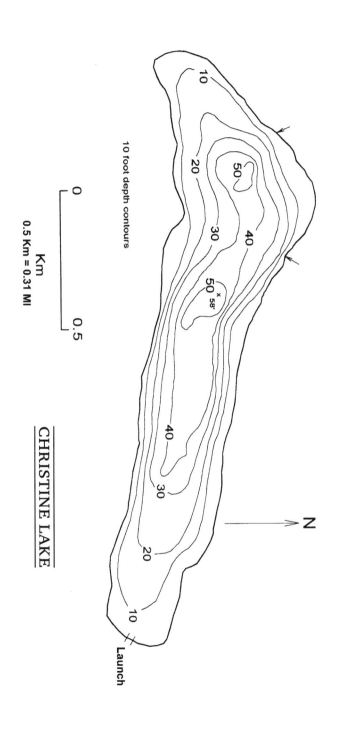

CHRISTINE LAKE

10 foot depth contours

Km
0.5 Km = 0.31 MI

N

Launch

Clarksville Pond

Clarksville

ACRES: 25

MAX DEPTH: 15'   **MEAN DEPTH:** 5'

CLARITY: 12'   **ELEVATION:** 2027'

FISH SPECIES: Brook Trout, Horned Pout

ACCESS: A gravel launch with a good turnaround. There is adequate parking for 4–5 vehicles.

DIRECTIONS: From the intersection of Route 45 and Clarksville Pond Road (by the school), take Clarksville Pond Rd. east for 1.0 mi. to access area on the right.

COMMENTS: Gas motors are not allowed on the pond. Clarksville Pond is a *Fly Fishing Only* pond.

Brook Trout, also known as "squaretail" or "speckled trout," require well-oxygenated cold water, 68 degrees or colder. They are found in meadow brooks, rivers, streams and ponds, and are easily caught with flies or small spinners. Earthworms are the best live bait for catching "brookies."

SOURCE: NH FISH & GAME

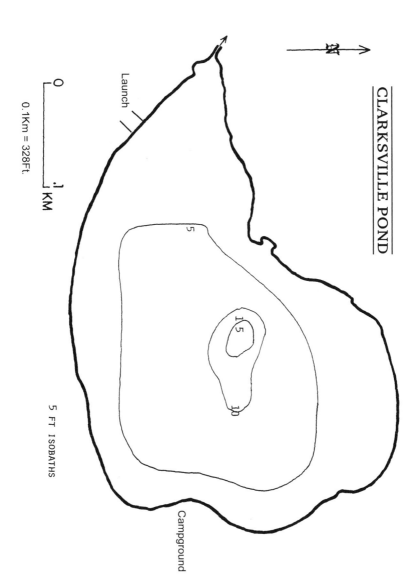

CLARKSVILLE POND

N

Launch

Campground

5

15

10

0   KM
0.1Km = 328Ft.

5 FT ISOBATHS

First Connecticut Lake

Pittsburg

ACRES: 2807

MAX DEPTH: 163' **MEAN DEPTH:** 56'

CLARITY: 12' **ELEVATION:** 1631'

FISH SPECIES: Salmon, Lake Trout

ACCESS: A nice paved ramp next to the dam.

DIRECTIONS: Launch is located on the southern tip of the lake next to the dam and is visible from Route 3.

COMMENTS: This is the largest of the three Connecticut Lakes. The Connecticut Lakes are being managed for Lake Trout and rules for Lake Trout and/or Salmon Lakes apply.

When a Brown Trout grows to about 12 inches in length, it feeds almost entirely on baitfish during twilight and nighttime hours. Live bait, spinners, and flies fished at dusk are equally effective to catch brown trout.

SOURCE: NH FISH & GAME

FIRST CONNECTICUT LAKE

PITTSBURG

Launch

LEGEND

X = INTERMEDIATE DEPTHS
R = ROCK STREWN LAKE BOTTOM

SCALE

2000 1000 0 2000 4000 feet

Contour interval 20 feet

Second Connecticut Lake

Pittsburg

ACRES: 1286

MAX DEPTH: 63'   **MEAN DEPTH:** 20'

CLARITY: 9'   **ELEVATION:** 1871'

FISH SPECIES: Brook Trout, Salmon, Lake Trout

ACCESS: A gravel launch area with ample parking.

DIRECTIONS: From the dam at the southern tip of First Connecticut Lake, go north 7.5 mi. to access road on the right. Follow this road for 0.5 mi. and take another right to the launch area.

COMMENTS: This lake is stocked with Landlocked Salmon and rules for Lake Trout and/or Salmon Lakes apply.

Lost fish strikes could be the sign of a dull hook.
A sharp hook should scratch your fingernail
while being lightly dragged across it.

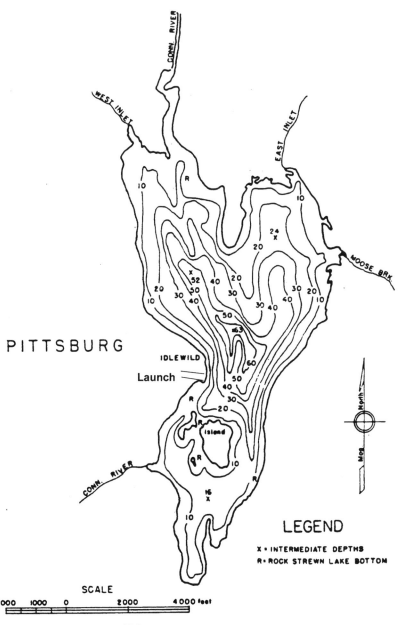

PITTSBURG

IDLEWILD

Launch

North

Mag

LEGEND

X = INTERMEDIATE DEPTHS
R = ROCK STREWN LAKE BOTTOM

SCALE

2000   1000   0   2000   4000 feet

Contour interval 10 feet

SECOND CONNECTICUT LAKE

Third Connecticut Lake

Pittsburg

ACRES: 289

MAX DEPTH: 100' **MEAN DEPTH:** 42'

CLARITY: 20' **ELEVATION:** 2191'

FISH SPECIES: Rainbow Trout, Lake Trout

ACCESS: A good gravel launch area with parking for 8–10 vehicles.

DIRECTIONS: From Moose Falls Campground on Route 3, travel north 3.6 mi. The boat access is on your left.

COMMENTS: This is the smallest of the three Connecticut Lakes. There is no shoreline development. Rules for Lake Trout and/or Salmon Lakes apply.

If you are a "catch and release" fishermen, remember that time is of the essence, so be sure to play and release the fish as carefully as possible. Remember also to keep the fish in the water as long as possible and handle it as little as possible from removing the hook.

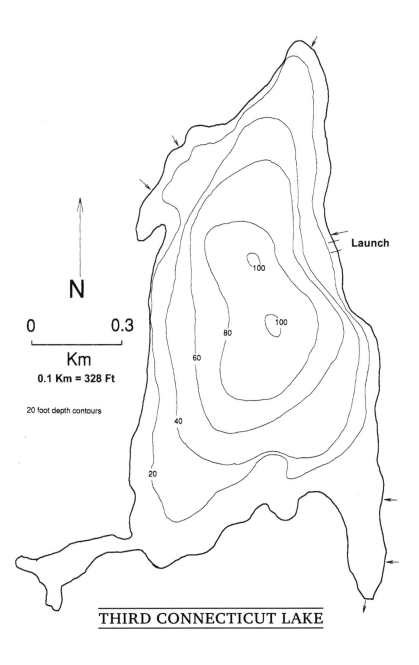

N

0   0.3

Km

0.1 Km = 328 Ft

20 foot depth contours

100

100

80

60

40

20

Launch

THIRD CONNECTICUT LAKE

Diamond Pond

Stewartstown

ACRES: 179

MAX DEPTH: 108' **MEAN DEPTH:** 36'

CLARITY: 12' **ELEVATION:** 2190'

FISH SPECIES: Brook Trout, Rainbow Trout, Lake Trout

ACCESS: A steep gravel launch area with parking for 4–6 vehicles.

DIRECTIONS: From Colebrook, take Route 26 east for 6.7 mi. Turn left onto Diamond Pond Road and proceed 5.5 mi. to Coleman State Park (see directions to Little Diamond Pond). From park entrance, continue on 1.2 mi. to boat access on left.

COMMENTS: A nice pond with moderate shoreline development. Rules for Lake Trout and/or Salmon Lakes apply.

Find a sticker that illustrates your favorite fishing knots and affix it to your tackle box for a quick reference . . . poor knots lose fish!

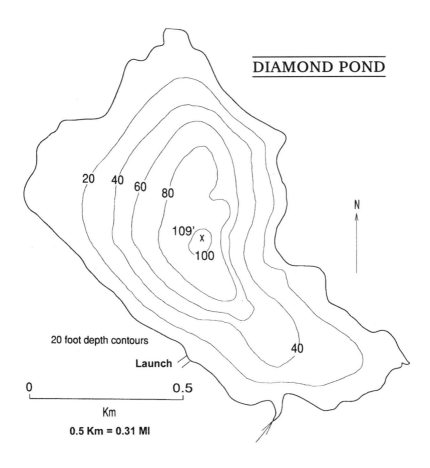

DIAMOND POND

20   40 60 80

109' x
100

40

N

20 foot depth contours

Launch

0   0.5

Km

0.5 Km = 0.31 MI

Little Diamond Pond

Stewartstown

ACRES: 53

MAX DEPTH: 15'   **MEAN DEPTH:** 6'

CLARITY: 7'   **ELEVATION:** 2249'

FISH SPECIES: Brook Trout, Rainbow Trout

ACCESS: A nice gravel launch with parking for 8–10 vehicles.

DIRECTIONS: From Colebrook, take Route 26 east for 6.7 mi.. Turn left onto Diamond Pond Road and proceed 5.5 mi. to Coleman State Park and fishing access on southwest shore of pond.

COMMENTS: A nice and very scenic pond with abundant wildlife and fine fishing. There is a 10-horsepower limit on motors.

> *If fish will follow your lure to the boat but won't strike, it might be that your line is too visible. Thin, clear monofilament line is almost invisible in the water at smaller diameters. If fishing for Brook Trout or fish up to four pounds, 4-pound test line should work fine.*

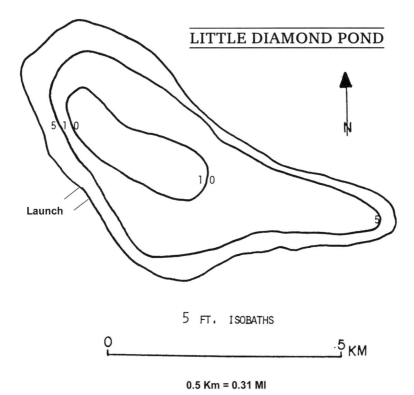

LITTLE DIAMOND POND

N

Launch

5 FT. ISOBATHS

0 — .5 KM

0.5 Km = 0.31 MI

Fish Pond

Columbia

ACRES: 21

MAX DEPTH: 8'   **MEAN DEPTH:** 5'

CLARITY: 7'   **ELEVATION:** 1395'

FISH SPECIES: Brook Trout, Rainbow Trout, Largemouth Bass

ACCESS: A new gravel launch and parking area. Watch for submerged rocks just off the ramp.

DIRECTIONS: From the intersection of Routes 3 and 26 in Colebrook, take Route 3 south 1.4 mi. to Fish Pond Road on the left. Go 2.2 mi. to access ramp on the right.

COMMENTS: A minimally developed small pond in the heart of the North Country.

When fishing with either spoons or spinners, try different depths until fish are found. A good rule of thumb is that an average ¼ oz. spoon will sink at a rate of about one foot per second. Count down your lure and note the depth you have success at.

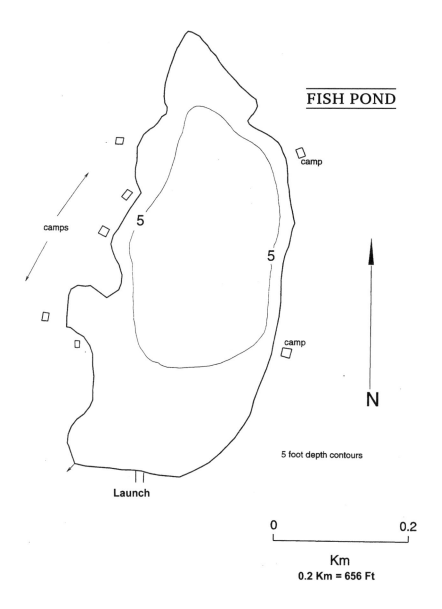

FISH POND

camp

camps

5

5

camp

Launch

N

5 foot depth contours

0   0.2

Km
0.2 Km = 656 Ft

Lake Francis

Clarksville

ACRES: 2051

MAX DEPTH: 85'   **MEAN DEPTH:** 44'

CLARITY: 13'   **ELEVATION:** 1385'

FISH SPECIES: Rainbow Trout, Brown Trout, Salmon, Lake Trout, Pickerel

ACCESS: There is a ramp and parking for 8–10 vehicles just off Route 3. There is also an access ramp at Lake Francis State Park.

DIRECTIONS: From the center of Pittsburg, follow Route 3 north 1.3 mi. to access area on the right. The entrance to Lake Francis State Park is another 5 mi. north on Route 3 and is well marked.

COMMENTS: Lake Francis is managed for Late Trout and rules for Lake Trout and/or Salmon Lakes apply.

> *When fishing in the summer when the mosquitoes are out, try not to wear red clothing, it seems to attract them.*

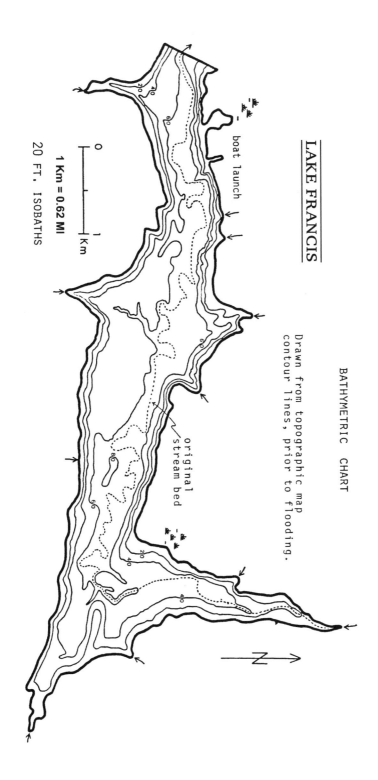

LAKE FRANCIS

BATHYMETRIC CHART

Drawn from topographic map
contour lines, prior to flooding.

boat launch

original
stream bed

N

1 Km = 0.62 MI

20 FT. ISOBATHS

0   1
|————————|
Km

Long Pond

Errol

ACRES: 47

MAX DEPTH: 11'   **MEAN DEPTH:** 4'

CLARITY: 7'   **ELEVATION:** 1405'

FISH SPECIES: Brook Trout

ACCESS: A natural earth launch area at the end of a short narrow drive. There is parking on the side of the road

DIRECTIONS: From the Intersection of Routes 26 and 16 in Errol, take Route 16 north 2.9 mi. to a narrow drive on the left. From here it is just 100 yards to water

COMMENTS: This is a quiet little pond, good for canoes or car top boats.

On cloudy days, or early or late in the day, copper, gold or brass-colored lures work best. On bright sunny days, choose a nickel finish.

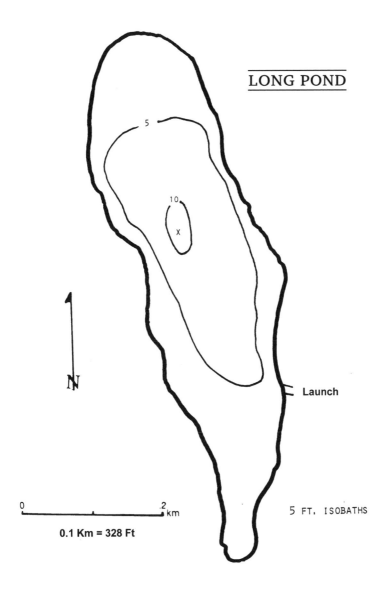

LONG POND

5

10

X

↑
N

Launch

0   .2 km

0.1 Km = 328 Ft

5 FT. ISOBATHS

Martin Meadow Pond

Lancaster

ACRES: 118

MAX DEPTH: 30'   **MEAN DEPTH:** 13'

CLARITY: 10'   **ELEVATION:** 1068'

FISH SPECIES: Rainbow Trout, Smallmouth Bass, Largemouth Bass, Pickerel, Horned Pout

ACCESS: A gravel launch with plenty of good turnaround space. There is adequate parking for 4–8 vehicles.

DIRECTIONS: From the Weeks State Park access road off Route 3 between Lancaster and Whitefield, head south 0.5 mi. to Martin Meadow Pond Road on your right. Follow this road 1.2 mi. to boat launch on the right.

COMMENTS: There is minimal shoreline development on Martin Meadow Pond. The pond is stocked with Rainbow Trout.

To encourage the fish to strike, try to vary the rate you retrieve the lure. Twitch the rod tip from time to time to give the lure a more erratic action.

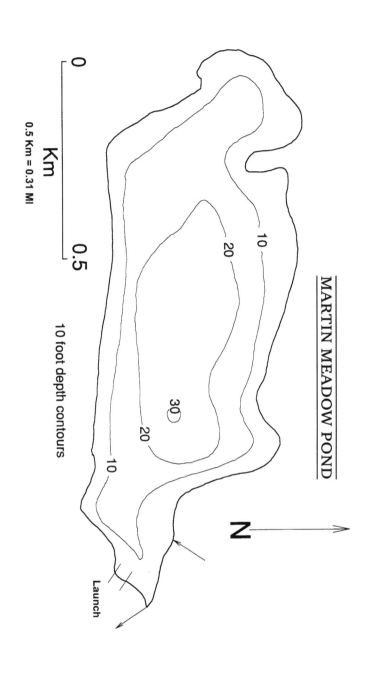

MARTIN MEADOW POND

N

Launch

Km
0.5 Km = 0.31 MI

0

0.5

10 foot depth contours

10

20

30

20

10

Mirror Lake

ACRES: 43

MAX DEPTH: 23'   **MEAN DEPTH:** 8'

CLARITY: 10'   **ELEVATION:** 1035'

FISH SPECIES: Brook Trout, Rainbow Trout, Brown Trout, Largemouth Bass, Pickerel, Horned Pout

ACCESS: A good gravel launch with parking for 10–12 vehicles.

DIRECTIONS: From the intersection of Routes 3 and 116 in Whitefield village, take Route 3 north for 1.0 mi. The access road to the lake is on the left (Log Cabin Rd).

COMMENTS: The access road is long and narrow, with a poor turnaround area for trailers. The pond is regularly stocked with Brook Trout and Rainbow Trout.

If you are having trouble getting an active worm on the hook, place it in your cupped hand and give it a quick clap. This will temporarily stun the worm.

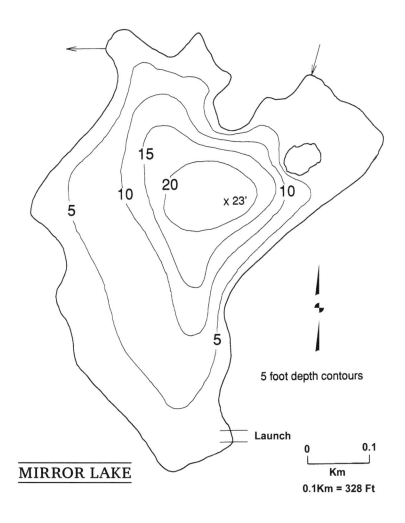

15

10 20

5 x 23' 10

5

5 foot depth contours

Launch

MIRROR LAKE

0   0.1
Km
0.1Km = 328 Ft

South Pond

ACRES: 124

MAX DEPTH: 95'   **MEAN DEPTH:** 44'

CLARITY: 32'   **ELEVATION:** 1115'

FISH SPECIES: Brook Trout, Rainbow Trout, Lake Trout, Smallmouth Bass, Largemouth Bass, Pickerel, Horned Pout

ACCESS: The launch area for canoes and car top boats is found at the USFS South Pond Recreation Area.

DIRECTIONS: From the covered bridge in Stark village, follow Route 110 east 3.4 mi. to the entrance to the South Pond Recreation Area.

COMMENTS: This is a pleasant pond stocked with Brook and Rainbow Trout. It is also handicap accessible. The pond lies within the boundaries of the White Mountain National Forest.

To get a twist out of your line, let it drag (without lure) behind a boat moving at trolling speed.

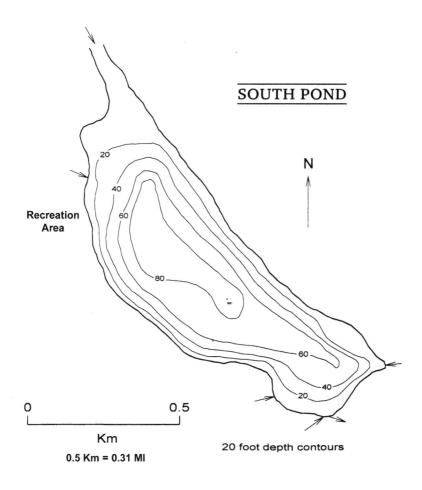

SOUTH POND

N

Recreation
Area

20

40

60

80

60

40

20

0   0.5

Km

0.5 Km = 0.31 MI

20 foot depth contours

Success Pond

ACRES: 245

MAX DEPTH: 25' **MEAN DEPTH:** 14'

CLARITY: 10' **ELEVATION:** 1600'

FISH SPECIES: Brook Trout, Rainbow Trout, Brown Trout, Smallmouth Bass, Largemouth Bass

ACCESS: A gravel launch with a good turnaround. There is parking for 3–4 vehicles with room for more on the side of the road.

DIRECTIONS: From Route 16, just south of Berlin's main business district, take the truck route north around the city. Success Pond Road is a dirt road across from the log yard for the mill, just past the dump. It is marked with a sign for OHRV Parking. The boat launch is 12 mi. up the road on the west side of the pond.

COMMENTS: It's a haul to get here but the fishing is pretty good. The shoreline is moderately developed.

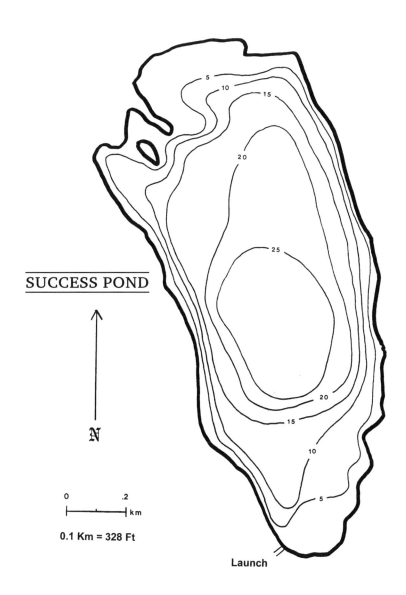

SUCCESS POND

N

0   .2

⊢───┴───⊣ km

0.1 Km = 328 Ft

Launch

South Pond in Stark

Akers Pond in Erroll

Clarksville Pond in Clarksville

Back Lake in Pittsburg

Cedar Pond in Milan

Success Pond in Success

Christine Lake in Stark

Mirror Lake in Whitefield

Grafton County

Lake Tarleton in Piermont

Lake Armington

ACRES: 142

MAX DEPTH: 32' **MEAN DEPTH:** 12'

CLARITY: 19' **ELEVATION:** 1334'

FISH SPECIES: Rainbow Trout, Brown Trout, Smallmouth Bass, Pickerel, Horned Pout

ACCESS: A good gravel boat launch with parking for 3–4 vehicles.

DIRECTIONS: Take Route 25C north from Warren. Just before reaching the Piermont town line (signed), take a left. (There's also a state boat launch sign marking the turn.) On gravel road, stay right at "Y" intersection and go another 0.1 mi. to the ramp.

COMMENTS: This is a pretty lake with minimal development along its shores. Lake Armington is stocked with Rainbow Trout.

When you notice a school of bait fish feeding on the surface, cast or troll close to the edges of it. Trout wait underneath the school for weak or injured fish to be left lagging as the school shifts and feeds.

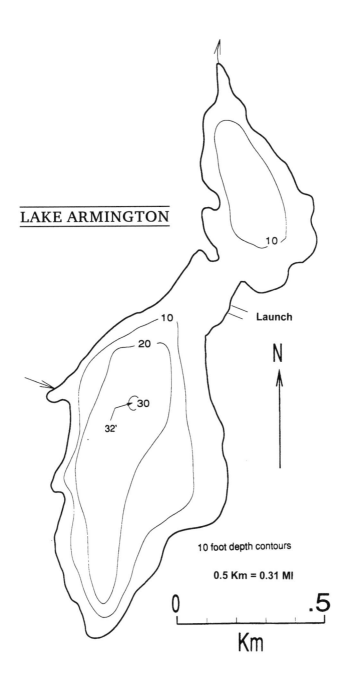

LAKE ARMINGTON

Launch

N

10

20

30

32'

10

10 foot depth contours

0.5 Km = 0.31 MI

0 .5

Km

Crystal Lake

Enfield

ACRES: 365

MAX DEPTH: 54' **MEAN DEPTH:** 21'

CLARITY: 12' **ELEVATION:** 890'

FISH SPECIES: Rainbow Trout, Smallmouth Bass, Pickerel

ACCESS: A nice gravel launch with parking for 8–10 vehicles.

DIRECTIONS: From Exit 17 off I-89, take Route 4 east 1.6 mi. to Route 4A. Turn right onto Route 4A and continue south 5.6 mi. to Crystal Lake Road on the left. Follow road straight ahead, avoiding road to right at 0.3 mi. At 0.7 mi, turn right onto Algonquin Road and continue 0.6 mi. to access area.

COMMENTS: Another nice pond with a moderately developed shoreline. Crystal Lake is stocked with Rainbow Trout.

If you don't plan on keeping the day's catch, remove your lure's hook barbs by pinching them with needlenose pliers. This will make for an easier release.

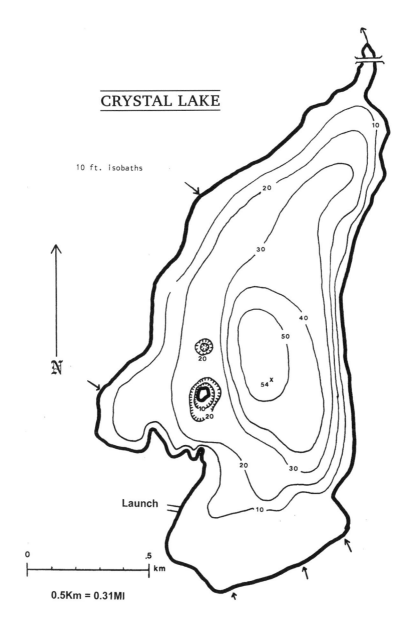

CRYSTAL LAKE

10 ft. isobaths

N

Launch

0   .5
km

0.5Km = 0.31MI

Echo Lake

Franconia

ACRES: 28

MAX DEPTH: 38'   **MEAN DEPTH:** 17'

CLARITY: 21'   **ELEVATION:** 1931'

FISH SPECIES: Brook Trout

ACCESS: A gravel launch with plenty of parking.

DIRECTIONS: From Franconia Notch Parkway (I-93), take Exit 34B and follow signs to Cannon Mountain Ski Area and Aerial Tramway. Go to northernmost parking lot in front of Tramway. Access ramp is on the right at the end of the lot.

COMMENTS: Echo Lake offers one of the better pond fishing opportunities in the White Mountains region. The lake is stocked with Brook Trout and is situated entirely within Franconia Notch State Park.

> *One of the best spots for Landlocked Salmon early in the spring is the mouth of a stream where smelt are spawning.*

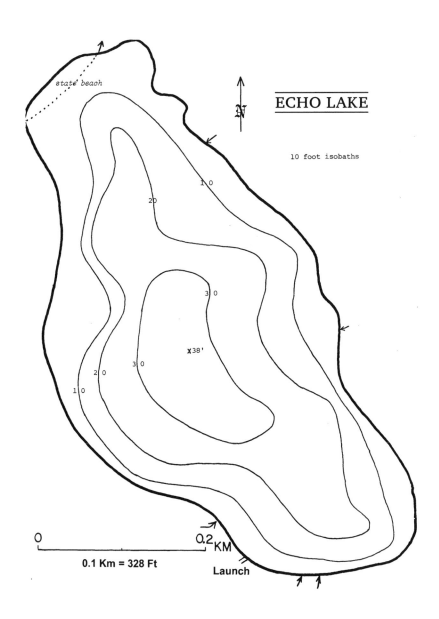

ECHO LAKE

10 foot isobaths

state beach

N

20

10

30

30

X 38'

20

10

0   0.2 KM

0.1 Km = 328 Ft

Launch

Little Squam Lake

Holderness

ACRES: 408

MAX DEPTH: 72' **MEAN DEPTH:** 32'

CLARITY: 25' **ELEVATION:** 562'

FISH SPECIES: Rainbow Trout, Salmon, Lake Trout, Smallmouth Bass, Pickerel, Horned Pout

ACCESS: A double concrete ramp with parking for 25 vehicles with trailers.

DIRECTIONS: In Holderness, at the intersection of Routes 3/25 and 113, take Route 113 north 0.3 mi. The ramp is on the right, parking is on the left. (The ramp is next door to the Science Center).

COMMENTS: The ramp is located on the causeway between Little Squam and Squam Lake. Rules for Lake Trout and/or Salmon Lakes apply.

Before heading out for a day of fishing, check your line for signs of nicks or abrasions. While trying to land a fish is not the time to be wondering how good your line is.

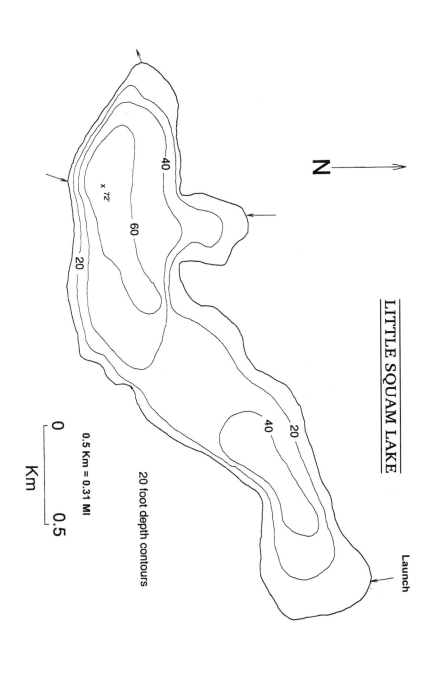

LITTLE SQUAM LAKE

N

20 foot depth contours

0.5 Km = 0.31 MI

0   0.5

Km

Launch

x 72'

40

60

20

40

20

Long Pond

ACRES: 93

MAX DEPTH: 7'   **MEAN DEPTH:** 5'

CLARITY: Very Clear   **ELEVATION:** 2170'

FISH SPECIES: Brook Trout, Rainbow Trout

ACCESS: Gravel ramp with parking for 10–15 vehicles.

DIRECTIONS: From the westernmost intersection of Routes 112 and 116 in Easton, turn onto Route 116 west (crossing bridge over Wild Ammonoosuc River) and drive 1.7 mi. to North-South Road on left. Continue 2.5 mi. to road (right) into USFS Long Pond Recreation Area. Follow for 0.5 mi. to pond.

COMMENTS: Very clear water, and fishing is surprisingly good considering the pond's shallow depth. Long Pond is located within the boundaries of the White Mountain National Forest.

> *Standing in a boat when fishing can frighten fish.*
> *Also dropping gear on the floor of the boat, creating*
> *a loud noise, can send them running for cover.*

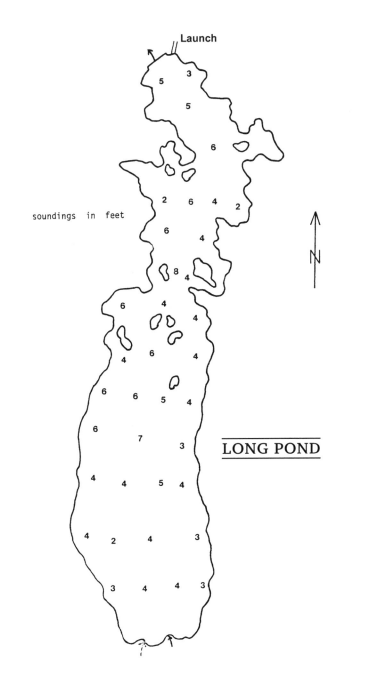

Launch

soundings in feet

N

LONG POND

Mascoma Lake

Enfield

ACRES: 1115

MAX DEPTH: 68'   **MEAN DEPTH**: 30'

CLARITY: 9'   **ELEVATION**: 751'

FISH SPECIES: Rainbow Trout, Brown Trout, Smallmouth Bass, Largemouth Bass, Pickerel, Horned Pout, White Perch

ACCESS: The north ramp is very good with parking for 6–8 vehicles. South ramp is also good, with parking for 12–15 vehicles.

DIRECTIONS: From Exit 17 off I-89, take Route 4 east 1.6 mi. to Route 4A on the right. Follow Route 4A 0.5 mi. to access ramp on your left. Travel 1.8 mi. further and second access ramp is located near Shaker Bridge.

COMMENTS: The shoreline is quite developed and the lake can be a busy place in the summer. All in all, though, there's good fishing here.

If you plan on keeping worms in a can overnight, add bits of egg shell and used coffee grounds to feed them. Also keep the dirt moist.

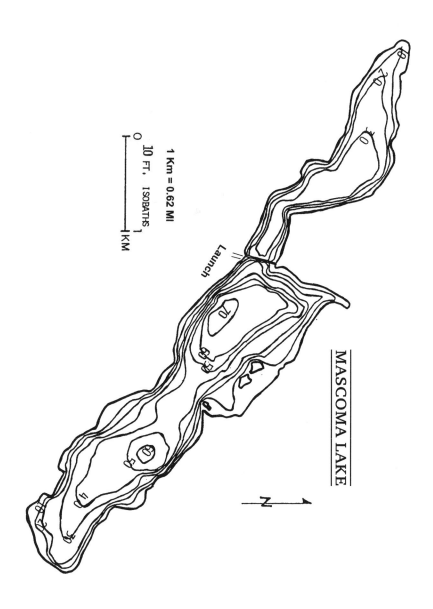

MASCOMA LAKE

N →

Launch

1 Km = 0.62 MI

10 FT. ISOBATHS

O ————————— KM

Moore Reservoir

Littleton

ACRES: 3490

MAX DEPTH: 147'   **MEAN DEPTH:** 52'

CLARITY: 11'   **ELEVATION:** 700'

FISH SPECIES: Brook Trout, Rainbow Trout, Brown Trout, Smallmouth Bass, Largemouth Bass, Pickerel, Horned Pout, Tiger Trout

ACCESS: There are two ramps here and both have excellent concrete ramps. There is parking for 6–8 vehicles at the Hilltop Road ramp and parking for 12–15 vehicles at the Old Waterford Road ramp.

DIRECTIONS: (*For Hilltop Road*) Take Exit 43 off I-93 and go south 0.1 mi. to the junction of Routes 18 and 135. Turn right onto Route 18 and continue 0.9 mi. to Hilltop Road on right. Follow Hilltop Road for 1.8 mi., then turn left onto gravel road to access ramp.

(*For Old Waterford Road*) From Exit 43, go north on Route 135 and take first left onto Old Waterford Road. Follow 1.9 mi. to end of road and access ramp.

COMMENTS: Moore Reservoir is an impoundment of the Connecticut River and is home to a large hydroelectric power facility. In Mid-June, the Littleton Trout Tournament is held here.

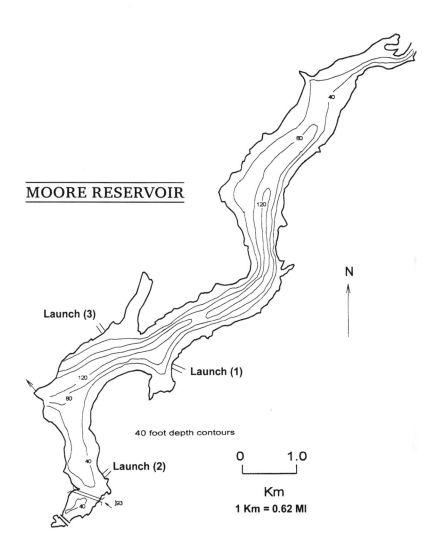

MOORE RESERVOIR

Launch (3)

Launch (1)

Launch (2)

40 foot depth contours

N

0   1.0

Km
1 Km = 0.62 MI

Newfound Lake

Bristol

ACRES: 4106

MAX DEPTH: 182'   **MEAN DEPTH**: 74'

CLARITY: 31'   **ELEVATION**: 586'

FISH SPECIES: Rainbow Trout, Salmon, Lake Trout, Whitefish, Smallmouth Bass, Pickerel, Horned Pout

ACCESS: A new boat ramp is located at Wellington State Park. There is a large parking area and rest rooms

DIRECTIONS: From the center of Bristol, take Route 3A north 2.3 mi. and turn left onto West Shore Road. Continue 2.1 mi. to Wellington State Park and follow signs to the ramp area.

COMMENTS: The fishing here is better than average. Rules for Lake Trout and/or Salmon Lakes apply. The minimum length for Lake Trout is 15". Newfound Lake is stocked with both Landlocked Salmon and Rainbow Trout.

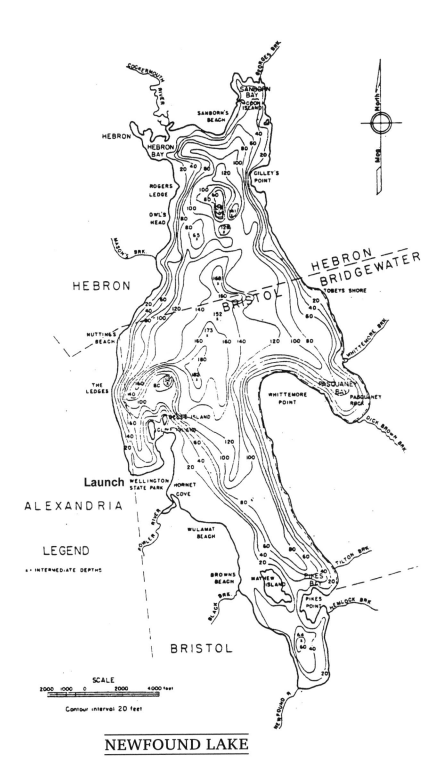

NEWFOUND LAKE

Oliverian Pond

Benton

ACRES: 32

MAX DEPTH: 13'   **MEAN DEPTH:** 7'

CLARITY: 3'   **ELEVATION:** 850'

FISH SPECIES: Brook Trout

ACCESS: A good cement boat ramp.

DIRECTIONS: From Glencliff, follow Route 25 north 1.6 mi. to access road on the right. Continue 0.5 mi. to the boat ramp.

COMMENTS: This is a small, but productive lake, amply stocked with Brook Trout.

As studies have shown that some freshwater fish in New Hampshire contain varying levels of mercury and pose a potential health risk, it is recommended that the following fish consumption guidelines be followed:

- *Pregnant and nursing women, and women who may get pregnant, can safely eat one 8-oz. meal per month of freshwater fish.*
- *Children under age 7 can safely eat one 3-oz. meal per month of freshwater fish.*
- *All other adults and children age 7 or older can safely eat four 8-oz. meals per month of freshwater fish.*

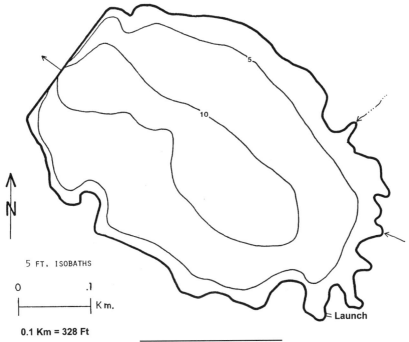

N

5 FT. ISOBATHS

0   .1

|———————| K m.

0.1 Km = 328 Ft

Launch

OLIVERIAN POND

Pearl Lake

Lisbon

ACRES: 62

MAX DEPTH: 21'   **MEAN DEPTH:** 10'

CLARITY: 18'   **ELEVATION:** 1017'

FISH SPECIES: Rainbow Trout, Smallmouth Bass, Pickerel, Horned Pout

ACCESS: There is a canoe or car top launch at both areas shown on the accompanying map.

DIRECTIONS: From the intersection of Routes 302 and 117 between Littleton and Lisbon, go south on Route 302 for 2.2 mi., then turn left onto Landaff Road. After crossing a former rail-road grade, turn left onto Pearl Lake Road. At 2.35 mi., veer right at "Y" intersection at west end of lake and proceed 0.15 mi. or 0.25 mi. to pull-offs on the left.

COMMENTS: This is a nice, quiet pond stocked with Rainbow Trout.

> *Organize your hooks and swivels on safety pins. This makes a handy dispenser and keeps them together.*

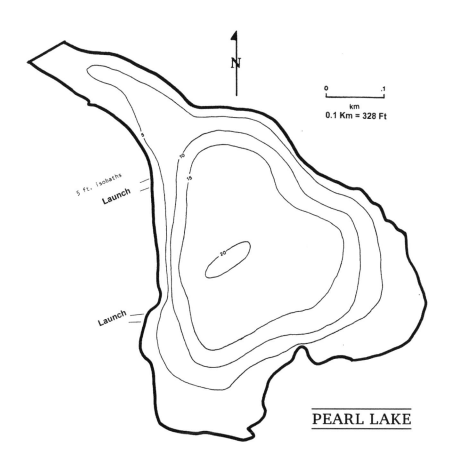

PEARL LAKE

Profile Lake

Franconia

ACRES: 15

MAX DEPTH: 16'   **MEAN DEPTH**: 8'

CLARITY: 12'   **ELEVATION**: 1925'

FISH SPECIES: Brook Trout

ACCESS: The north shore of the lake is limited to walk-in access only. There is, however, a small boat launch at the south end of the pond.

DIRECTIONS: Walk-in access is available from either of the "Old Man" parking and viewing areas near Cannon Mountain Ski Area and Exit 34B on the Franconia Notch Parkway (I-93). To reach the boat launch at the south end of the lake, go south 0.6 mi. from Parkway Exit 34B and turn into the parking area (marked "Trailhead Parking"), where there's a small launch for canoes and boats on the right.

COMMENTS: This is a *Fly-Fishing Only* pond. Profile Lake is located in Franconia Notch State Park. No motorized boats are allowed on the lake.

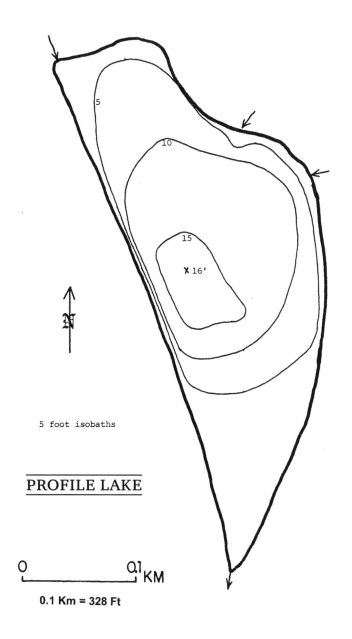

5 foot isobaths

PROFILE LAKE

0   0.1 KM

0.1 Km = 328 Ft

Russell Pond

Woodstock

ACRES: 39

MAX DEPTH: 74'   **MEAN DEPTH:** 33'

CLARITY: 37'   **ELEVATION:** 1648'

FISH SPECIES: Brook Trout

ACCESS: A paved ramp with parking for 8–12 vehicles.

DIRECTIONS: From I-93 in Woodstock, take Exit 31 and proceed east on Tripoli Road (closed during the winter and early spring) for 1.8 mi., where Russell Pond Road enters on the left. Follow steep and winding road 2.8 mi. to parking area at north shore of pond.

COMMENTS: Russell Pond is located entirely within the White Mountain National Forest and is a nice, deep and clear pond. Motorized boats are prohibited on its waters. Access is located within the grounds of the USFS Russell Pond Campground.

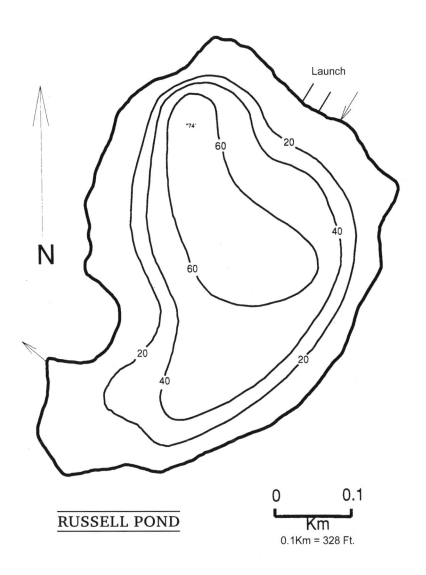

N

Launch

·74·
60
20
40
60
20
40
20

RUSSELL POND

0   0.1
Km
0.1Km = 328 Ft.

Spectacle Pond

Groton

ACRES: 46

MAX DEPTH: 39'   **MEAN DEPTH:** 12'

CLARITY: 21'   **ELEVATION:** 820'

FISH SPECIES: Brook Trout, Rainbow Trout

ACCESS: A nice launch site with parking for 4–8 vehicles

DIRECTIONS: From the center of Groton village at the intersection of Groton and North Groton Roads, follow North Groton Road 1.0 mi. and turn right. Continue 0.1 mi. to lake.

COMMENTS: This is a very scenic pond. Motorized boats are prohibited.

"Finding fish" is a matter of knowing where fish are most comfortable. Look for the species' favorite kinds of underwater structure, temperature zones and places that they will "feel safe" from predators — fish are nature's food for many creatures!

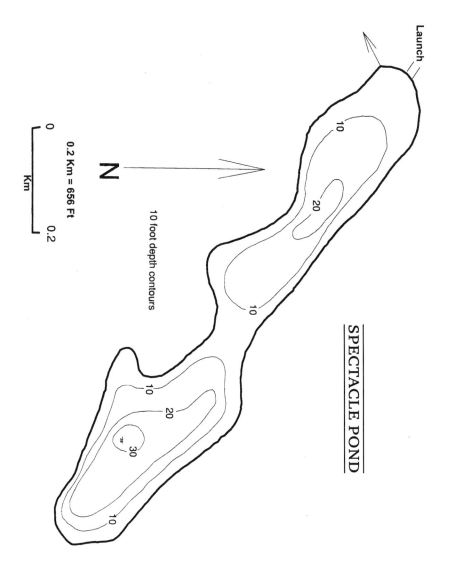

SPECTACLE POND

Launch

10 foot depth contours

N

0.2 Km = 656 Ft

0   0.2
Km

Stinson Lake

Rumney

ACRES: 350

MAX DEPTH: 72'   **MEAN DEPTH:** 35'

CLARITY: 15'   **ELEVATION:** 1303'

FISH SPECIES: Brook Trout, Rainbow Trout, Lake Trout, Smallmouth Bass, Pickerel, Horned Pout

ACCESS: A gravel launch with adequate turnaround and parking for 5–6 vehicles.

DIRECTIONS: From I-93 in Plymouth, take Exit 26 and go west on Route 25 for 7.4 mi. before turning right toward Rumney village. Continue straight ahead for 5.0 mi on Stinson Lake Road and veer left at fork at south end of lake. Continue 0.1 mi. to access on the right.

COMMENTS: The pond is stocked with Rainbow Trout and provides good fishing. The shoreline is heavily developed. This is the largest body of water within the proclamation boundary of the White Mountain National Forest.

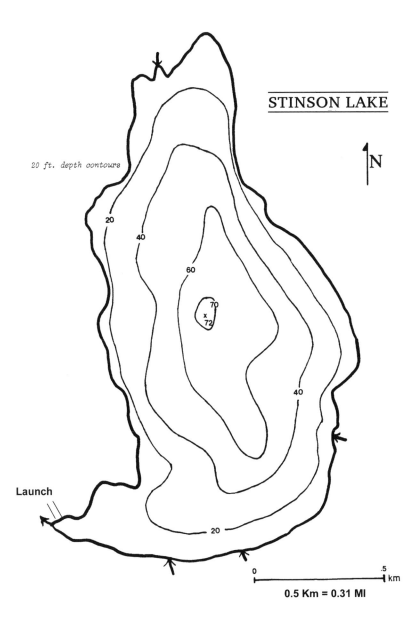

STINSON LAKE

N

20 ft. depth contours

20

40

60

70
x
72

40

40

Launch

20

0   .5
                     km

0.5 Km = 0.31 MI

Streeter Pond

Sugar Hill

ACRES: 68

MAX DEPTH: 20'   **MEAN DEPTH:** 8'

CLARITY: 8'   **ELEVATION:** 914'

FISH SPECIES: Brook Trout, Rainbow Trout, Brown Trout

ACCESS: Gravel ramp.

DIRECTIONS: From Exit 38 (Franconia village) on I-93, go north on Route 18/116 for 1.3 mi. to Streeter Pond Road on your left. Continue 2.1 mi. The access road is on the right.

COMMENTS: This is a shallow pond with lightly stained water. There is moderate shoreline development.

In the summertime, fishing is best in the first light of morning, especially if the surface of the water is dead calm and there is a slight fog on it. The same holds true for just before dark if the same conditions can be found.

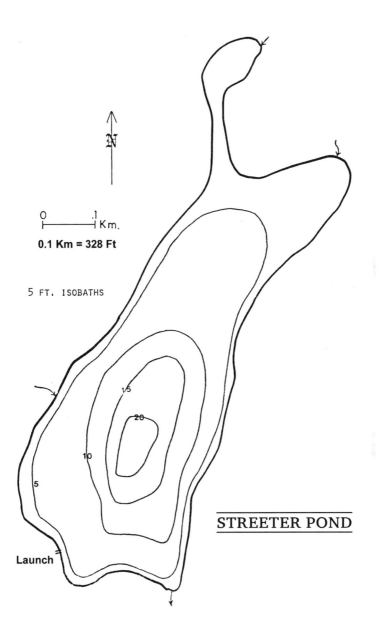

0.1 Km = 328 Ft

5 FT. ISOBATHS

STREETER POND

Launch

Lake Tarleton

Piermont

ACRES: 315

MAX DEPTH: 66' **MEAN DEPTH:** 28'

CLARITY: 10' **ELEVATION:** 1305'

FISH SPECIES: Rainbow Trout, Brown Trout, Lake Trout, Smallmouth Bass, Pickerel, Horned Pout

ACCESS: A dirt ramp with parking for 5–8 vehicles.

DIRECTIONS: From the junction of Routes 25 and 25c in Warren, take Route 25c for 5.1 miles. The boat access is on the right at the southeast corner of the lake.

COMMENTS: Lake Tarleton, situated on the edge of White Mountain National Forest, has little shoreline development and is stocked with Rainbow and Brook Trout.

> *Fishing for large trout is generally more productive on dark cloudy days than bright sunny ones. It's best to fish clear sunny days either early in the morning or late in the afternoon.*

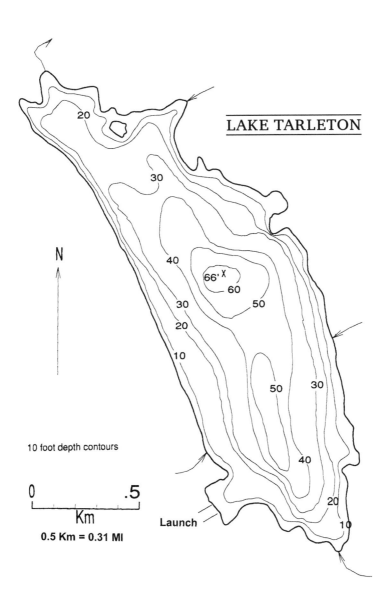

LAKE TARLETON

N

10 foot depth contours

0 ————————— .5
Km
0.5 Km = 0.31 MI

Launch

Tewksbury Pond

Grafton

ACRES: 46

MAX DEPTH: 50' **MEAN DEPTH:** 27'

CLARITY: 15' **ELEVATION:** 913'

FISH SPECIES: Brook Trout, Rainbow Trout, Brown Trout, Horned Pout

ACCESS: A fairly new concrete ramp with paved parking for 10 vehicles.

DIRECTIONS: From Grafton Center, proceed west on Route 4 for 2.5 mi. to Tunnel Road on the left. The access road to the pond is reached (on the left) in 0.2 mi.

COMMENTS: The access road looks like a steep driveway. There is good fishing here for stocked trout. No motors are allowed.

Brook Trout have a delicate skin in place of scales. Please always wet your hands before touching them; dry handling may remove part of their protective layer of slime and can cause a fatal infection to develop.

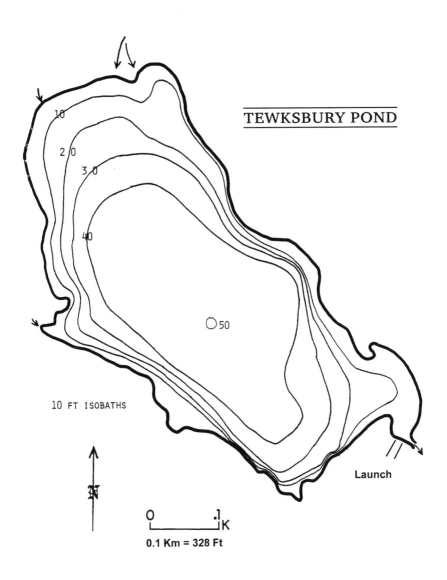

TEWKSBURY POND

10 FT ISOBATHS

10

20

30

40

50

N

O   .1 K

0.1 Km = 328 Ft

Launch

Profile Lake in Franconia

Tewksbury Pond in Grafton

Echo Lake in Franconia

Russell Pond in Woodstock

Carroll County

Chocorua Lake in Tamworth

Basin Pond

Chatham

ACRES: 29

MAX DEPTH: 13'   **MEAN DEPTH:** 4'

CLARITY: 10'   **ELEVATION:** 662'

FISH SPECIES: Brook Trout

ACCESS: The pond is located on the eastern edge of the White Mountain National Forest, adjacent to the "Basin Campground." There is a paved ramp with available parking for 15–20 vehicles. Parking is shared with a nearby picnic area.

DIRECTIONS: From Route 302 in Fryeburg, Maine, follow Route 113 north for 18.9 mi. to the turnoff (on left) into the WMNF Basin Campground. Follow this paved road 0.6 mi. to a large parking lot on the right.

COMMENTS: A very scenic pond, great for canoeing and kayaking. This area has a wheelchair-accessible fishing dock and picnic area.

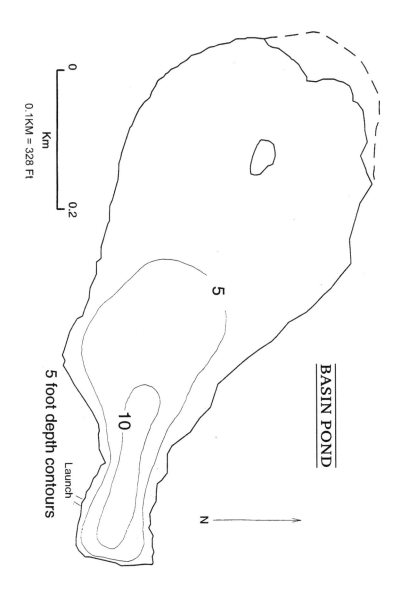

BASIN POND

N

Km
0.1KM = 328 Ft

0

0.2

5 foot depth contours

5

10

Launch

Chocorua Lake

Tamworth

ACRES: 222

MAX DEPTH: 29'   **MEAN DEPTH:** 12'

CLARITY: 19'   **ELEVATION:** 573'

FISH SPECIES: Brown Trout, Smallmouth Bass, Pickerel, Horned Pout, White Perch

ACCESS: A shallow launch from the eastern shoreline, good for car tops and canoes. There is adequate parking for 10–15 vehicles.

DIRECTIONS: From the intersection of Routes 16 and 113 in Chocorua village, follow Route 16 north 1.6 mi. The entrance to Chocorua Park is signed and on the left.

COMMENTS: No motor-powered boats are allowed. The lake is one of the most photographed in the state, with picturesque Mount Chocorua providing a dramatic backdrop to the northwest.

The state record Rainbow Trout was 35.5 inches in length and weighed in at 15 lbs. 7.2 oz. It was caught in the Pemigewasset River in Bristol on Sept. 16, 1996, by Granite State angler Lance King.

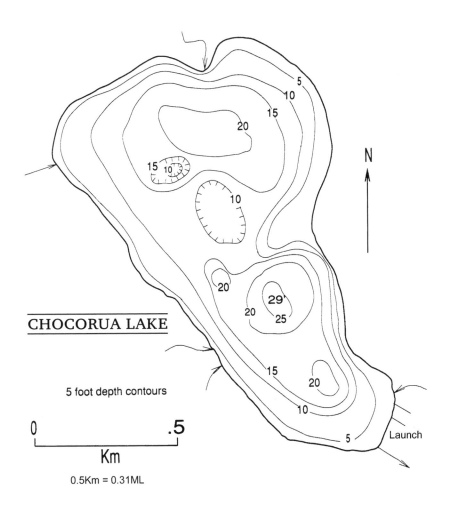

CHOCORUA LAKE

5 foot depth contours

0   .5

Km

0.5Km = 0.31ML

Conner Pond

Ossipee

ACRES: 87

MAX DEPTH: 58' **MEAN DEPTH:** 29'

CLARITY: 35' **ELEVATION:** 899'

FISH SPECIES: Brook Trout

ACCESS: A shallow, narrow launch located off the side of the road suitable for canoes, car tops and small trailers. One hundred yards further down the road there is a larger ramp where a fee is charged.

DIRECTIONS: From the intersection of Routes 16 and 25 in West Ossipee, follow Route 16/25 south for 2.5 mi. Turn right onto Pine Hill Road. Drive 3.7 mi. to boat launch on the right.

COMMENTS: This is a nice, clear water pond with minimal shoreline development. Conner Pond is stocked with Brook Trout. There is a 10 mph speed limit for boats on the pond. The state is planning to build a new ramp on the east shore. Take the first right at the pond and you should see signs marking the spot.

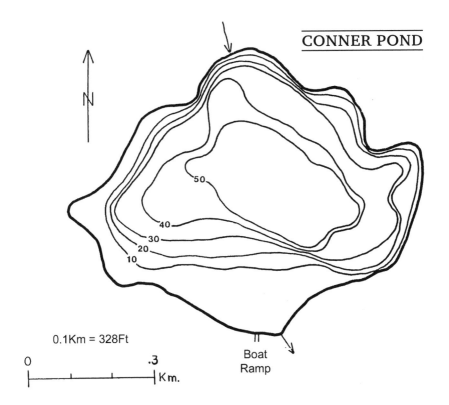

CONNER POND

N

50
40
30
20
10

0.1Km = 328Ft

0   .3

Km.

Boat
Ramp

Conway Lake

ACRES: 1298

MAX DEPTH: 49'   **MEAN DEPTH:** 20'

CLARITY: 25'   **ELEVATION:** 437'

FISH SPECIES: Rainbow Trout, Brown Trout, Smallmouth Bass, Largemouth Bass, Pickerel, Horned Pout

ACCESS: A concrete ramp with parking for 10–15 vehicles across the road.

DIRECTIONS: From the intersection of Routes 16, 113, and 153 in Conway village, follow Route 113 east 3.3 mi. to Mill Street on the right. Take Mill Street 0.8 mi. to the boat access next to the dam at the lake's north end. The access ramp is right next to a small town beach.

COMMENTS: Rules for Lake Trout and or Salmon Lakes apply on Conway Lake.

According to the N.H. Fish and Game Department, in recent years 60 percent of all boating fatalities in the state have been alcohol-related. For obvious reasons, don't operate a boat if impaired (intoxicated).

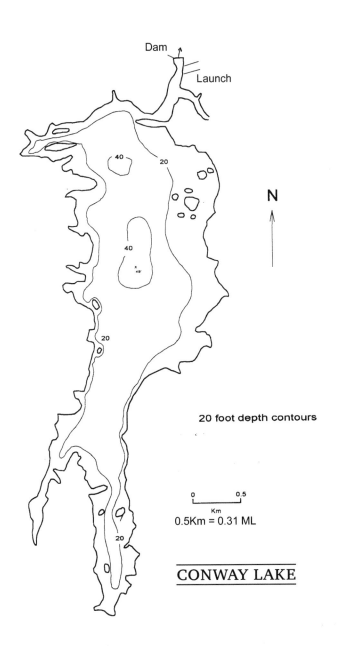

Dam

Launch

N

40 20

40

X
49'

20

20 foot depth contours

20

0   0.5

Km
0.5Km = 0.31 ML

20

CONWAY LAKE

Upper Hall Pond

Sandwich

ACRES: 23

MAX DEPTH: 43′ **MEAN DEPTH:** 12′

CLARITY: 15′ **ELEVATION:** 1587′

FISH SPECIES: Brook Trout

ACCESS: A sand and gravel launch with parking for 8–10 vehicles.

DIRECTIONS: From the intersection of Routes 175 and 49 in Campton, follow Route 49 north 3.2 mi. to Sandwich Notch Road (a dirt road, sometimes on the rough side) on your right. Go 2.3 mi. to access road on the right. From here it's a steep 0.2 mi. to the pond.

COMMENTS: The access is definitely on the rough side, but it's adequate for canoe and car top boats. Hall Pond is a *Fly Fishing Only* pond.

Lake Trout are a prize game fish because of their size and power. It is not at all unusual for anglers to catch lakers in the 3 to 6 pound range. Ideally, lake trout live in water at or near 50 degrees, and are generally found on or near the bottom of the water body.

SOURCE: NH FISH & GAME

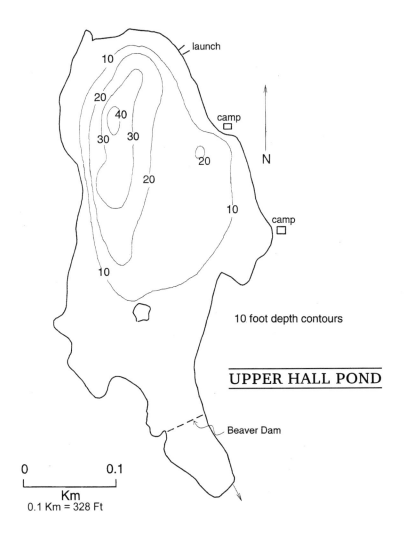

launch

camp

N

camp

10

20

40

30 30

20

20

10

10

10 foot depth contours

UPPER HALL POND

Beaver Dam

0   0.1

Km

0.1 Km = 328 Ft

Horn Pond

Wakefield

ACRES: 198

MAX DEPTH: 30' **MEAN DEPTH:** 13'

CLARITY: 23' **ELEVATION:** 554'

FISH SPECIES: Rainbow Trout, Brook Trout, Brown Trout, Smallmouth Bass, Largemouth Bass, Pickerel, Horned Pout, Bluegill

ACCESS: An excellent boat ramp on the Maine side of the pond near the dam. There is adequate parking for 10–15 vehicles.

DIRECTIONS: From the intersection of Routes 109 and 153 in Sanbornville, take Route 109 east for 5.5 mi. to the Maine border and turn left into the access area.

COMMENTS: This is a well-stocked pond with minimal shoreline development.

Throughout New Hampshire, approximately 60 remote ponds are stocked with fingerling brook trout. Due partly to light fishing pressure at these ponds, the trout tend to live longer and grow more than brookies found in small streams and rivers.

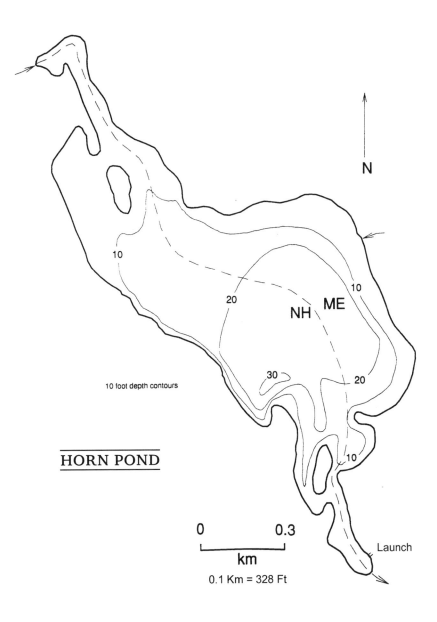

N

10

10

20

ME

NH

30

20

10

10 foot depth contours

HORN POND

0   0.3

km

0.1 Km = 328 Ft

Launch

Little Pond

Sandwich

ACRES: 19

MAX DEPTH: 27' **MEAN DEPTH:** 12'

CLARITY: 15' **ELEVATION:** 650'

FISH SPECIES: Brook Trout, Largemouth Bass, Pickerel, Horned Pout

ACCESS: A dirt launch, a bit on the narrow side, but fine for the size of boats allowed on the pond.

DIRECTIONS: From Route 109 in Sandwich village, take Little Pond Road east 0.6 mi. to the boat access on the left.

COMMENTS: No motor-powered boats are allowed. Little Pond Road runs along the east side of the pond.

In early spring, multitudes of suckers come up from the depths in search of running currents in which to spawn at stream and river mouths. Their antics are clearly visible by virtue of their numbers. Trout will flock to the area and gorge themselves on the sucker eggs, and can often be enticed with similar bait or contrasting lures.

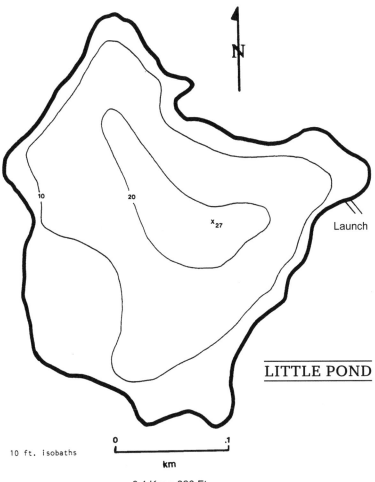

10   20   X₂₇

N

Launch

LITTLE POND

10 ft. isobaths

0   .1

km

0.1 Km = 328 Ft

Loon Lake

Freedom

ACRES: 192

MAX DEPTH: 53'   **MEAN DEPTH:** 24'

CLARITY: 23'   **ELEVATION:** 388'

FISH SPECIES: Brook Trout, Rainbow Trout, Smallmouth Bass, Pickerel, Horned Pout

ACCESS: A rutted, shallow dirt launch. Vehicles are required to park along the side of the road.

DIRECTIONS: From the intersection of Routes 153 and 25 (1.7 mi. east of Effingham Falls), where the highway crosses over the Ossipee River, follow Route 25 east for 0.6 mi. and turn left onto a dirt road. Go 0.3 mi to the access area on the right.

COMMENTS: There is moderate shoreline development on the lake.

Trout will be found at different depths according to their preference to temperature: Brook Trout, not higher than 68 degrees; Brown Trout, 65–75 degrees; Rainbow Trout, not higher than 65–68 degrees; Lake Trout, below 60–65 degrees; Landlocked Salmon, 50 degrees.

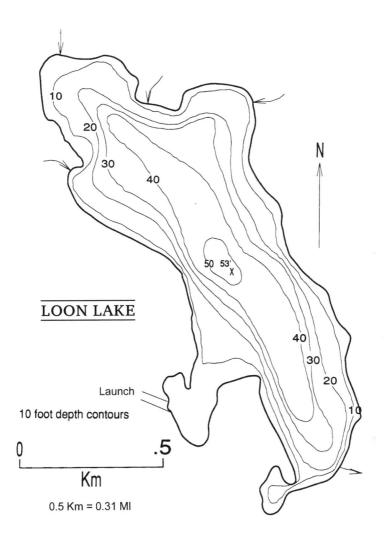

LOON LAKE

Launch

10 foot depth contours

0   .5

Km

0.5 Km = 0.31 MI

N

Lovell Lake

Wakefield

ACRES: 538

MAX DEPTH: 39' **MEAN DEPTH:** 17'

CLARITY: 15' **ELEVATION:** 570'

FISH SPECIES: Rainbow Trout, Brown Trout, Smallmouth Bass, Pickerel, Horned Pout, White Perch, Walleye

ACCESS: An old paved ramp off the side of road, with parking off site. Directions are posted on a sign at the ramp.

DIRECTIONS: From the intersection of Route 109 and 16 near Sanbornville, take Route 109 east 0.8 mi. to the access ramp on the right.

COMMENTS: There is heavy shoreline development along Lovell Lake. Needless to say, the lake can get quite busy at times.

In the spring, feeding trout will be near the surface. As the water starts to warm up with the summer approaching, the trout go deeper in search of the cooler thermal layers. Spring-fed lakes stay cool nearer the surface and will have some trout staying shallow all year.

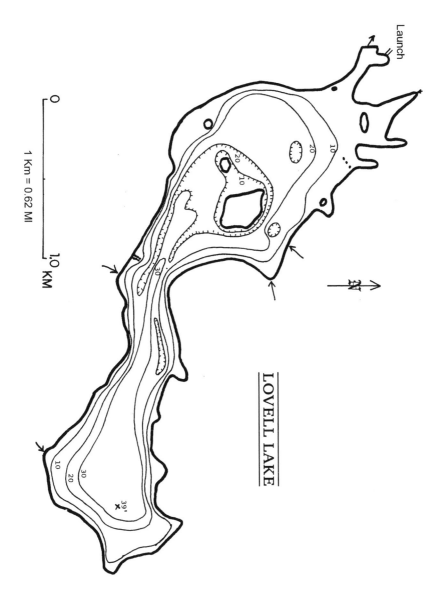

Launch

LOVELL LAKE

N

0   1.0 KM

1 Km = 0.62 MI

Ossipee Lake

Ossipee

ACRES: 3092

MAX DEPTH: 50'   **MEAN DEPTH:** 28'

CLARITY: 18'   **ELEVATION:** 406'

FISH SPECIES: Rainbow Trout, Brown Trout, Salmon, Lake Trout, Smallmouth Bass, Largemouth Bass, Pickerel, Horned Pout

ACCESS: A paved ramp near the bridge over Pine River, with parking for 20–25 vehicles.

DIRECTIONS: From the intersection of Routes 16 and 25 in Center Ossipee, take Route 25 east 0.5 mi. The launch and parking area are on the right.

COMMENTS: The launch facility is very nice. The lake is about one mile down the Pine River from the launch area. Rules for Lake Trout and/or Salmon Lakes apply.

The state record Lake Trout was 39.5 inches in length and weighed in at 28 lbs., 8 oz. It was caught in Newfound Lake in Bristol back on April 24, 1958, by Massachusetts angler Albert C. Staples.

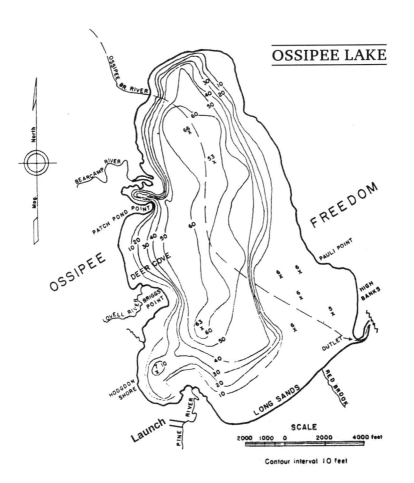

OSSIPEE LAKE

North

Mag. North

OSSIPEE BR RIVER

BEARCAMP RIVER

PATCH POND POINT

OSSIPEE

DEER COVE

LOVELL RIVER

BRIGGS POINT

HODGDON SHORE

Launch

PINE RIVER

LONG SANDS

FREEDOM

PAULI POINT

HIGH BANKS

OUTLET

RED BROOK

SCALE

2000 1000 0 2000 4000 feet

Contour interval 10 feet

Silver Lake

ACRES: 995

MAX DEPTH: 164'   **MEAN DEPTH:** 47'

CLARITY: 18'   **ELEVATION:** 466'

FISH SPECIES: Rainbow Trout, Lake Trout, Whitefish, Smallmouth Bass, Pickerel, Horned Pout

ACCESS: A good paved, concrete ramp with parking for 6–10 vehicles.

DIRECTIONS: From the intersection of Routes 41 and 113 in Madison, follow Route 41 south 2.7 mi. to East Shore Drive on the left. From the start of this road, it is 0.7 mi. to the boat access.

COMMENTS: This is a splendid lake to spend a day on. Rules for Lake Trout and/or Salmon Lakes apply.

Brown Trout, typically found in deep, quiet pools or slow-moving streams prefer living in water that is between 65 and 70 degrees. Brown Trout in New Hampshire are usually 7–14 inches long and weigh less than a pound. It is not unusual, though, to catch brown trout weighing 2–4 pounds. **SOURCE: NH FISH & GAME**

SILVER LAKE

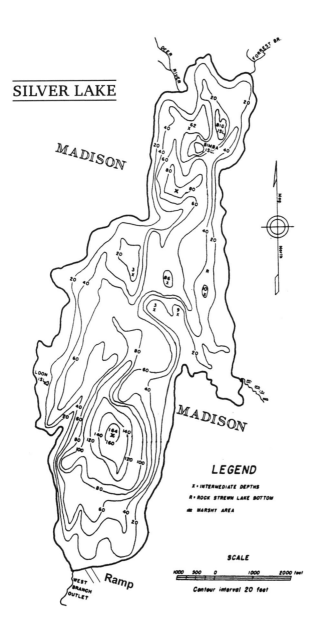

MADISON

MADISON

LEGEND

X = INTERMEDIATE DEPTHS
R = ROCK STREWN LAKE BOTTOM
≋ MARSHY AREA

SCALE

1000 500   0   1000   2000 feet

Contour interval 20 feet

Ramp

WEST BRANCH OUTLET

Lake Wentworth

Wolfeboro

ACRES: 3017

MAX DEPTH: 83' **MEAN DEPTH:** 21'

CLARITY: 21' **ELEVATION:** 534'

FISH SPECIES: Rainbow Trout, Smallmouth Bass, Pickerel, Horned Pout, White Perch

ACCESS: An excellent ramp with parking for 10–20 vehicles.

DIRECTIONS: From the center of Wolfeboro, follow Routes 109/28 east 0.7 mi. to access area. Look for the sign reading "Mast Landing." The access ramp is over a set of railroad tracks with a sharp drop-off down to the water. This ramp is difficult for larger rigs to access.

COMMENTS: The ramp actually lets you onto neighboring Crescent Lake, which is just south of Lake Wentworth.

The state record Brown Trout was 32.5 inches in length and weighed in at 16 lbs. 6 oz. Ken Reed Jr. of Connecticut caught it in the Connecticut River in Pittsburg on July 4, 1975.

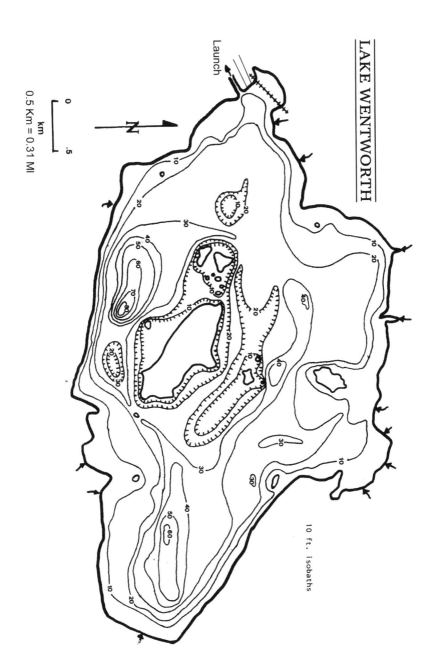

LAKE WENTWORTH

Launch

N

km
0.5 Km = 0.31 MI
0   .5

10 ft. isobaths

White Lake

ACRES: 123

MAX DEPTH: 48' **MEAN DEPTH:** 21'

CLARITY: 19' **ELEVATION:** 439'

FISH SPECIES: Brook Trout, Pickerel, Horned Pout

ACCESS: A sandy, gravel launch area with parking for 4–5 vehicles, with more available parking space on the side of the road.

DIRECTIONS: From the intersection of Routes 16 and 25 in West Ossipee, take Route 16 north for 0.6 mi. Turn left onto Depot Road and go 0.9 mi. to dirt access road on the right. Follow this road for 0.25 mi. to the pond.

COMMENTS: There are no homes or camps on the lake, which is located in White Lake State Park. There is a campground and beach on its southeastern shore. No motorboats are allowed on this *Fly Fishing Only* lake.

> *The state record Brook Trout was 25.5 inches in length and weighed in at 9 lbs. It was caught in Pleasant Lake in New London back on May 8, 1911, by New Hampshire angler A. Val Woodruff.*

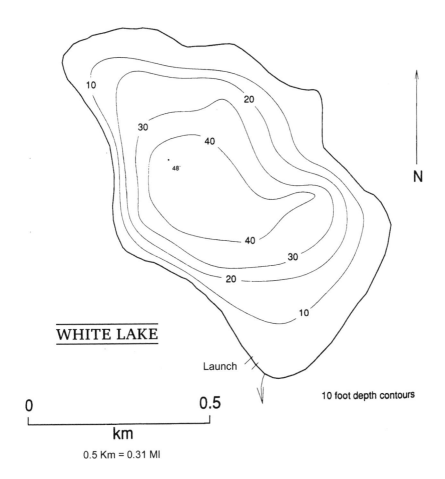

N

10

20

30

40

48'

40

30

20

10

WHITE LAKE

Launch

10 foot depth contours

0   0.5

km

0.5 Km = 0.31 MI

White Pond

Ossipee

ACRES: 47

MAX DEPTH: 37' **MEAN DEPTH:** 19'

CLARITY: 16' **ELEVATION:** 474'

FISH SPECIES: Brook Trout, Rainbow Trout

ACCESS: A small gravel ramp with parking for 2–4 vehicles.

DIRECTIONS: From the intersection of Routes 28 and 16 in Ossipee, take Route 16 south 1.7 mi. and turn left onto Granite Road. Go 0.35 mi. and turn left onto White Pond Road. Continue 0.65 mi. to the access ramp on the left.

COMMENTS: This is a *Fly Fishing Only* pond. There is a 6 mph speed limit for boats on White Pond.

Rainbow Trout thrive best in cold water, but have been known to live in waters with temperatures up to 77 degrees, if the water is aerated. In most streams and ponds, the rainbows are between 6 and 12 inches in length and usually weigh under a pound. Rainbows up to 3–5 pounds are not uncommon in larger lakes.

SOURCE: NH FISH & GAME

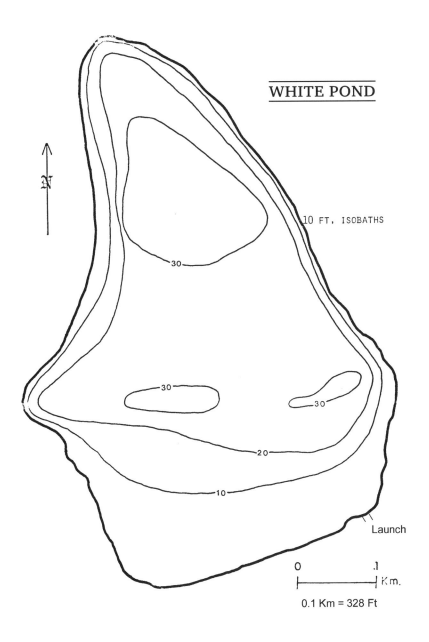

WHITE POND

N

10 FT. ISOBATHS

30

30

30

20

10

Launch

0   .1
|—————————————————| Km.

0.1 Km = 328 Ft

Horn Pond in Wakefield

White Pond in Ossipee

Wentworth Lake in Wolfeboro

Conner Pond in Ossipee

Basin Pond in Chatham

White Lake in Tamworth

Silver Lake in Madison

Little Pond in Sandwich

Sullivan and Cheshire Counties

Dublin Lake in Dublin

Center Pond

Nelson

ACRES: 36

MAX DEPTH: 36' **MEAN DEPTH:** 16'

CLARITY: 20' **ELEVATION:** 1410'

FISH SPECIES: Rainbow Trout, Brook Trout, Largemouth Bass, Horned Pout

ACCESS: A nice gravel ramp with parking for 8–12 vehicles.

DIRECTIONS: From the center of Nelson, follow Center Pond Road (across from the post office) west for 0.3 mi. The access road is on the left. From here it is 0.1 mi to the pond.

COMMENTS: This is a small, quiet pond with adequate parking. There are no motorboats allowed on its waters.

There are hundreds of New Hampshire lakes and ponds with restrictions on the use of motors, outboard motors, electric motors, and horse power. For a listing of the New Hampshire water bodies regulated with restrictions, visit the N.H. Division of Safety Services website at:
www.state.nh.us/safety/ss/bodies.html

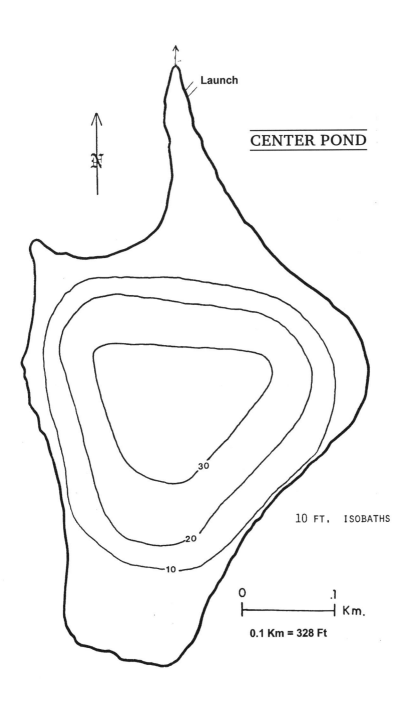

Launch

CENTER POND

30

20

10

10 FT. ISOBATHS

0   .1

Km.

0.1 Km = 328 Ft

Chapman Pond

Sullivan

ACRES: 20

MAX DEPTH: 17'   **MEAN DEPTH:** 7'

CLARITY: 8'   **ELEVATION:** 1330'

FISH SPECIES: Brook Trout

ACCESS: A gravel launch with parking for 3–4 vehicles.

DIRECTIONS: From the intersection of Route 9 and Center Street in East Sullivan (marked by a blinking traffic light), take Center Street for 2.3 mi and bear right at an intersection toward Sullivan village. In another 0.4 mi., turn right onto Gilsum Road and continue 0.4 mi. to a dirt road on the right. Take this for 0.7 mi., then turn right onto the access road. From here it's 0.2 mi. to the pond.

COMMENTS: This is a nice pond, though a little on the shallow side. There is no shoreline development and for the most part the water is protected from any strong winds.

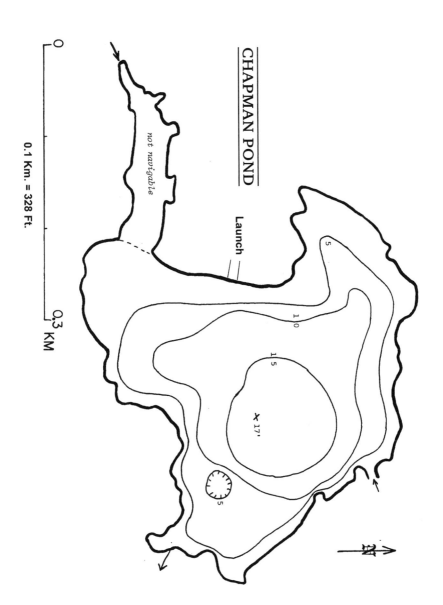

CHAPMAN POND

Launch

not navigable

5

10

15

✕ 17'

5

0

0.1 Km. = 328 Ft.

0.3 KM

Dublin Lake

Dublin

ACRES: 239

MAX DEPTH: 100'   **MEAN DEPTH:** 43'

CLARITY: 31'   **ELEVATION:** 1479'

FISH SPECIES: Brook Trout, Largemouth Bass, Horned Pout

ACCESS: A paved ramp, with parking for 6–8 vehicles along the side of the road.

DIRECTIONS: From the center of Dublin take Route 101 west for 1.5 mi. (Route 101 travels along the north side of the lake) to Lake Road on the left. Follow Lake Road as it passes along the west side of the lake. The launch is reached in 0.5 mi. and is on the left.

COMMENTS: This is a nice clear water pond with some good drops and depth. It's also a good trolling lake. There is a 10 mph speed limit except between 4 P.M. and one-half hour after sunset.

It is unlawful in the State of New Hampshire to release a fish in waters other than where it was caught. Fish must be returned to the water where they were taken.

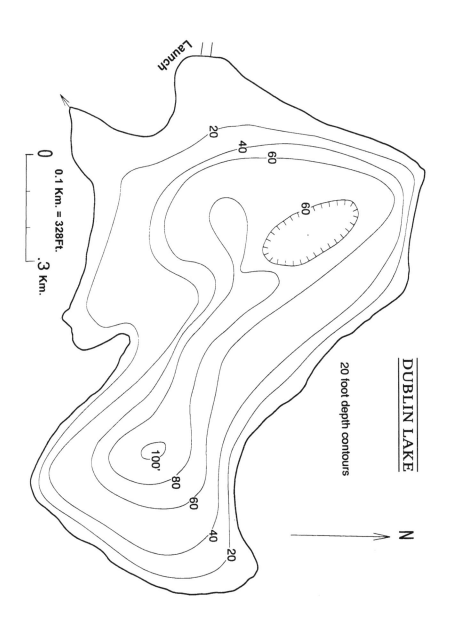

DUBLIN LAKE

20 foot depth contours

N

0.1 Km. = 328Ft.

0   .3 Km.

Launch

Gilmore Pond

Jaffrey

ACRES: 115

MAX DEPTH: 43'   **MEAN DEPTH:** 16'

CLARITY: 22'   **ELEVATION:** 1052'

FISH SPECIES: Brook Trout, Brown Trout, Smallmouth Bass, Largemouth Bass, Pickerel, Horned Pout, White Perch

ACCESS: A dirt ramp with a turnaround on the side of the road. There is parking for 3–4 vehicles alongside of the road.

DIRECTIONS: From the traffic light in the center of Jaffrey, take Route 202 south for 0.4 mi. and turn right onto Gilmore Pond Road. In 1.8 mi. bear right at a fork (staying on Gilmore Pond Road.) At 2.5 mi. you'll reach the launch on your right, along the side of the road.

COMMENTS: This is a very popular pond with a good variety and quantity of fish. Shoreline development is moderate.

GILMORE POND

Launch

10

20

30

40

×43

20

10

N

10 ft. depth contours

0.1 Km = 328 Ft

0   .1   .2   .3
km

Granite Lake

ACRES: 228

MAX DEPTH: 108'   **MEAN DEPTH:** 34'

CLARITY: 15'   **ELEVATION:** 1278'

FISH SPECIES: Rainbow Trout, Lake Trout, Smallmouth Bass, Pickerel, Horned Pout

ACCESS: A paved ramp with parking for 2–3 vehicles on the side of the ramp.

DIRECTIONS: From the intersection of Granite Lake Road and Route 9 (by state highway garage) in Nelson, follow Granite Lake Road 0.9 mi. to the launch on the right.

COMMENTS: This is a good trolling lake, especially in the spring. Parking is very limited.

On water bodies designated as "Fly-Fishing Only" ponds, the fishing season begins on the fourth Saturday in April and ends on October 15. In these ponds, the taking of brook trout, rainbow trout, lake trout, trout hybrids, and salmon between two hours after sunset and one hour before sunrise is prohibited.

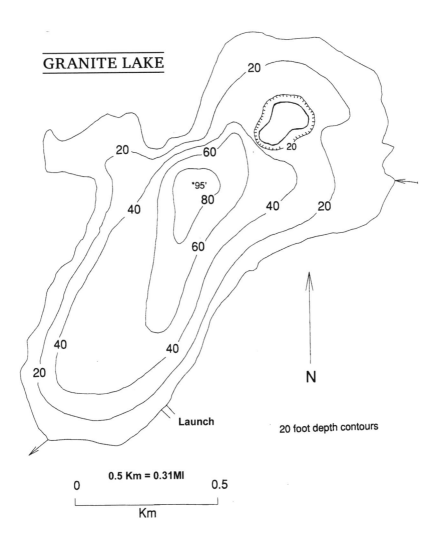

GRANITE LAKE

20

20

20

60

20

'95'
80

40

40

20

60

40

40

20

N

Launch

20 foot depth contours

0.5 Km = 0.31MI

0   0.5

Km

Laurel Lake

Fitzwilliam

ACRES: 155

MAX DEPTH: 44' **MEAN DEPTH:** 20'

CLARITY: 19' **ELEVATION:** 1099'

FISH SPECIES: Rainbow Trout, Brown Trout, Smallmouth Bass, Pickerel, Horned Pout

ACCESS: A paved ramp with parking for 6–8 vehicles.

DIRECTIONS: From Route 119 in Fitzwilliam Depot, take Laurel Lake Road south 2.4 mi. to the access ramp on the right.

COMMENTS: The pond has a wide paved ramp with parking along the side of the road. Stocking includes Brown and Rainbow Trout. Laurel Lake becomes a bit busy during peak weekend times in the summer.

If you are fishing from a boat, remember that state law requires one wearable life preserver for each person in the boat. Weak or non-swimmers should always wear an approved personal floatation device; children under 5 are required to wear an approved vest or jacket.

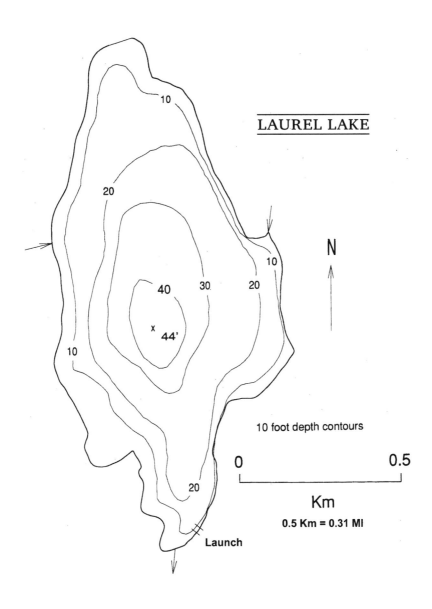

LAUREL LAKE

10 foot depth contours

0   0.5

Km

0.5 Km = 0.31 MI

Long Pond

Lempster

ACRES: 116

MAX DEPTH: 58'   **MEAN DEPTH:** 16'

CLARITY: 24'   **ELEVATION:** 1548'

FISH SPECIES: Brook Trout, Horned Pout

ACCESS: A gravel ramp with a nice turnaround. Tends to be a little shallow in the summer. There is parking for 6–8 vehicles across from launch.

DIRECTIONS: From the store on Route 31 in Washington, go north 0.1 mi. and turn left onto Lempster Mountain Road. In 2.5 mi., turn left onto Long Pond Road. Go 1.1 mi. to access on your right. The launch is next to the town beach.

COMMENTS: This is a nice pond with moderate shoreline development.

In New Hampshire, it is illegal to use or have in possession a set line, net, fishing otter, trawl, grapple, spear, jack, jack light, poisons, explosives or electrical device or any other device for killing or stunning fish, unless otherwise specifically permitted.

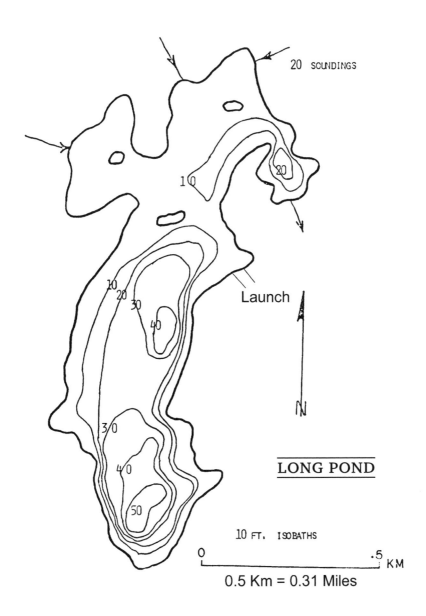

20 SOUNDINGS

Launch

N

LONG POND

10 FT. ISOBATHS

0   .5
|_____| KM

0.5 Km = 0.31 Miles

Millen Pond

Washington

ACRES: 156

MAX DEPTH: 41'   **MEAN DEPTH:** 16'

CLARITY: 25'   **ELEVATION:** 1582'

FISH SPECIES: Brook Trout, Rainbow Trout, Brown Trout, Smallmouth Bass, Pickerel, Horned Pout

ACCESS: A gravel ramp with a nice drop off. Some pavement remains, but this does not pose a problem. There is adequate parking for 4–6 vehicles.

DIRECTIONS: From the gazebo in Washington on Route 31, go south on Faxon Hill Road for 0.3 mi., then turn right onto Millen Pond Road. Proceed another 1.1 mi. to the access ramp on left.

COMMENTS: There is a daily 10 mph speed limit for boats on Millen Pond, except from 10 A.M. to noon and from 2:30–5:30 P.M.

Coldwater Species found in New Hampshire lakes and ponds include: Brook Trout, Rainbow Trout, Brown Trout, Landlocked Salmon, Lake Trout and Whitefish.

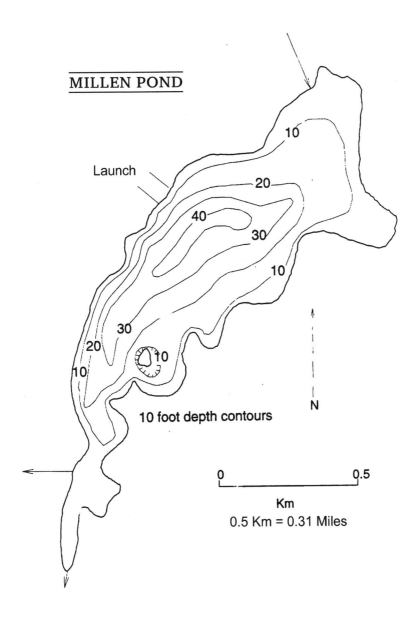

MILLEN POND

Launch

10

20

40

30

10

30

20

10

10

10 foot depth contours

N

0   0.5

Km

0.5 Km = 0.31 Miles

Nubanusit Lake

Hancock

ACRES: 715

MAX DEPTH: 100'   **MEAN DEPTH:** 38'

CLARITY: 41'   **ELEVATION:** 1376'

FISH SPECIES: Rainbow Trout, Brown Trout, Lake Trout, Smallmouth Bass, Pickerel, Horned Pout

ACCESS: A paved ramp with parking for 8–10 vehicles.

DIRECTIONS: From the intersection of Routes 123 and 137 in Hancock, take Route 123 north for 2.3 mi. and turn left. A sign here also marks the road for the "Harris Center." Go 0.6 mi. to a "T" and turn right. Continue for 1.1 mi. to the ramp area on the left.

COMMENTS: "Nubie" is a fine lake for trolling, although it can get windy out on the lake at times. Nubanusit is managed as a Lake Trout lake and rules for Lake Trout and/or Salmon Lakes apply.

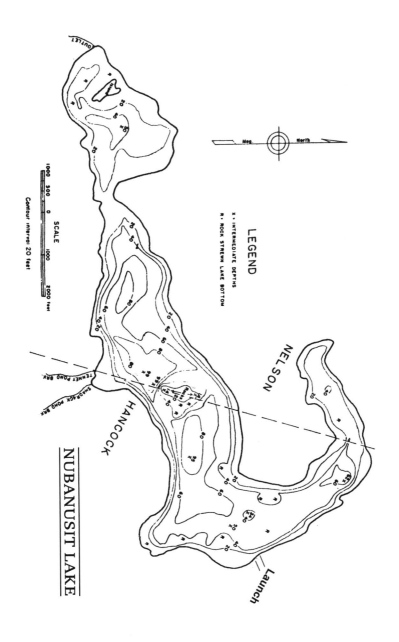

NUBANUSIT LAKE

LEGEND

X = INTERMEDIATE DEPTHS
R = ROCK STREWN LAKE BOTTOM

SCALE

Contour interval 20 feet

Mag.   North

NELSON

HANCOCK

OUTLET

Launch

Rand Pond

Goshen

ACRES: 39

MAX DEPTH: 27$'$ **MEAN DEPTH:** 11$'$

CLARITY: 11$'$ **ELEVATION:** 1257$'$

FISH SPECIES: Brook Trout, Rainbow Trout

ACCESS: A good boat launch, gravel into swallow water.

DIRECTIONS: From Route 31 in the center of Goshen (at blinking light), take Brook Road east, following signs to Rand Pond Campground. The launch area is 2.4 mi. on the left.

COMMENTS: The shoreline is densely packed with cottages. The boat launch is adjacent to a campground. Motorized boats are limited to 10 horsepower or less while on Rand Pond.

To qualify for a resident fishing license in New Hampshire, a person must have resided in the state for six months immediately prior to his or her applying for a license, and must not claim residency in any other state for any purpose.

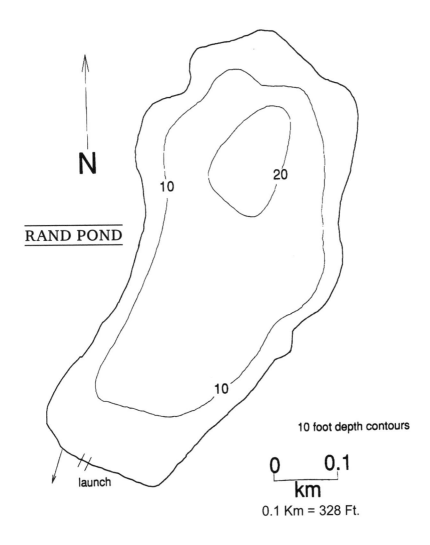

N

RAND POND

10

20

10

10 foot depth contours

0   0.1

km

0.1 Km = 328 Ft.

launch

Sand Pond

Marlow

ACRES: 211

MAX DEPTH: 60' **MEAN DEPTH:** 20'

CLARITY: 28' **ELEVATION:** 1543'

FISH SPECIES: Brook Trout, Brown Trout, Smallmouth Bass, Horned Pout

ACCESS: Features a new facility with a paved ramp and parking for eight vehicles with trailers.

DIRECTIONS: From the intersection of Routes 123 and 10 in Marlow, take Route 10 north 2.8 mi. to Sand Pond Road on the right. Follow Sand Pond Road 2.8 mi. to a fork. Veer right, and at 0.3 miles turn right again. The ramp is 0.4 mi. further on the left.

COMMENTS: This is a nice pond, with clear water. It is generally well stocked with Brook and Brown Trout. There is moderate development on the western shoreline.

> *Lake- and pond-dwelling trout often feed on schools of bait fish suspended at shallow depths; trout lurking near the bottom generally are resting, not feeding.*

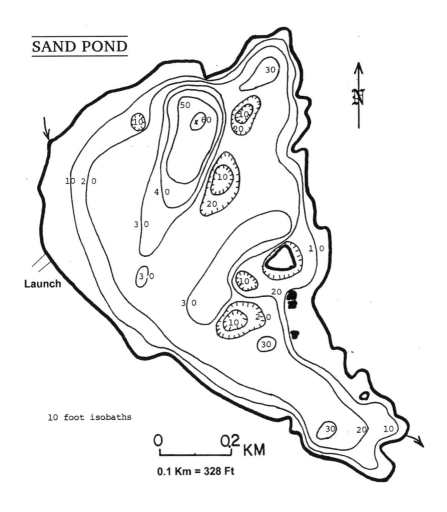

SAND POND

Launch

10 foot isobaths

0 ___ 0.2 KM

0.1 Km = 328 Ft

Silver Lake

Harrisville

ACRES: 333

MAX DEPTH: 85'   **MEAN DEPTH:** 36'

CLARITY: 27'   **ELEVATION:** 1319'

FISH SPECIES: Lake Trout, Rainbow Trout, Smallmouth Bass, Pickerel, Horned Pout

ACCESS: A paved ramp.

DIRECTIONS: From the center of Harrisville, take Main Street west to Nelson Road. Take Nelson Road north toward Nelson (staying left at fork at 0.8 mi.). In 1.9 mi., turn left onto Silver Lake Road. Go 1.1 mi. (passing Childs Pond or Bog on the left) to the Silver Lake access ramp on the right.

COMMENTS: This is a nice clear lake with good depth. There is moderate shoreline development. Silver Lake is managed for lake trout and rules for Lake Trout and/or Salmon Lakes apply.

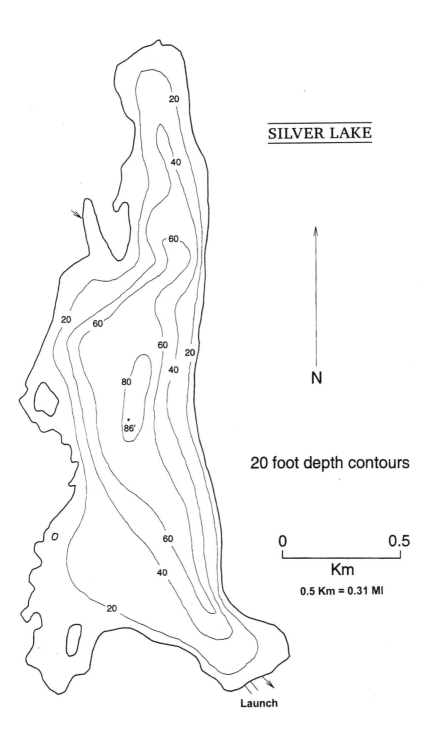

SILVER LAKE

N

20 foot depth contours

0   0.5

Km

0.5 Km = 0.31 MI

Launch

Smith Pond

Washington

ACRES: 27

MAX DEPTH: 31'   **MEAN DEPTH:** 16'

CLARITY: 18'   **ELEVATION:** 1075'

FISH SPECIES: Brook Trout, Brown Trout

ACCESS: A good gravel launch with parking for 6–8 vehicles.

DIRECTIONS: From the intersection of Routes 9 and 31 in Hillsborough Lower Village, take Route 31 north for 5.3 miles. Turn right onto Smith Pond Road and proceed 0.6 mi. to the launch on your right.

COMMENTS: A nice pond, but an overabundance of stunted perch can be more than annoying at times.

Fishing licenses issued in New Hampshire are valid January 1 through December 31 of the year in which they are issued. Lost licenses may be replaced at Fish and Game headquarters in Concord or at the original issuing agent for a small fee.

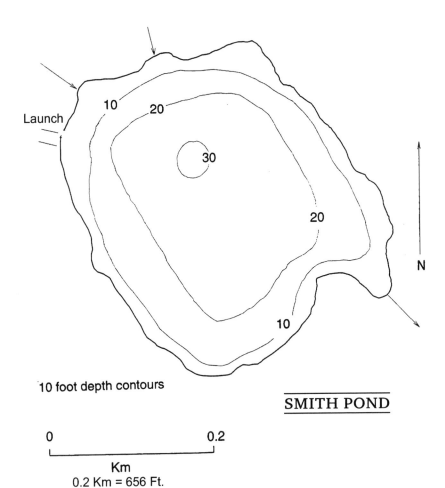

Launch

10   20

30

20

20

10

10 foot depth contours

SMITH POND

N

0   0.2

Km
0.2 Km = 656 Ft.

Spofford Lake

Chesterfield

ACRES: 707

MAX DEPTH: 64'   **MEAN DEPTH:** 30'

CLARITY: 34'   **ELEVATION:** 716'

FISH SPECIES: Rainbow Trout, Smallmouth Bass, Large-mouth Bass, Pickerel, Horned Pout, White Perch, Northern Pike

ACCESS: A paved ramp with good turnaround space. There is adequate parking for 8–10 vehicles.

DIRECTIONS: From the intersection of Routes 9 and 63, just north of Chesterfield village, follow Route 9 east (right) for 0.6 mi. and turn left onto Route 9a. Go 0.1 mi. The ramp is straight ahead.

COMMENTS: A good-sized pond with a healthy fish population. The daily limit on Brook, Brown, Rainbow Trout and their hybrids is two fish. The minimum length on Brook, Brown, Rainbow Trout is 15 inches. The island in Spofford Lake is a State Park.

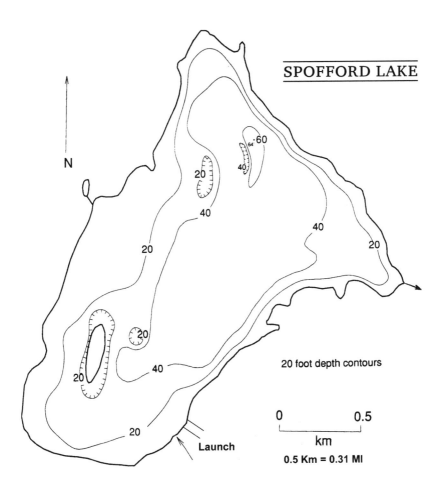

SPOFFORD LAKE

N

60

40

20

40

40

20

20

40

20

40

20

20

20

Launch

20 foot depth contours

0   0.5
km
0.5 Km = 0.31 MI

Spoonwood Lake

Nelson

ACRES: 144

MAX DEPTH: 66'   **MEAN DEPTH:** 28'

CLARITY: Slightly stained **ELEVATION:** 1386'

FISH SPECIES: Brown Trout, Smallmouth Bass, Large-mouth Bass, Pickerel, Horned Pout

ACCESS: A short portage from nearby Nubanusit Lake.

DIRECTIONS: (*To Nubanusit Lake ramp*) In Hancock, at the intersection of Routes 123 and 137, take Route 123 north for 2.3 mi. and turn left. Look here for a sign marking the way to the "Harris Center." Go 0.6 mi. to a "T" at Hunts Pond and turn right. Continue 1.1 mi. to ramp area on the left.

COMMENTS: The fishing here makes it well worth the portage from Nubanusit Lake. Motors are banned on Spoonwood Lake, with the exception of electric motors.

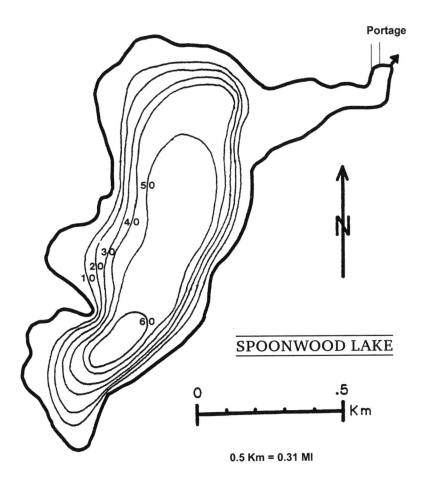

Portage

N

SPOONWOOD LAKE

0 ⸻ .5 Km

0.5 Km = 0.31 MI

Stone Pond

Marlborough

ACRES: 65

MAX DEPTH: 48' **MEAN DEPTH:** 20'

CLARITY: 20' **ELEVATION:** 1296'

FISH SPECIES: Brook Trout, Brown Trout, Smallmouth Bass, Horned Pout

ACCESS: A dirt launch with parking for 3–4 vehicles.

DIRECTIONS: In Marlborough, from the intersection of Routes 101 and 124, take Route 124 south for 0.1 mi. and turn left onto Pleasant Street. At 0.6 mi., go straight after a stop, then take the next left. At 0.3 mi., stay left and continue another 1.8 mi. to the boat launch on the left.

COMMENTS: The boat launch is right next to the town beach. The launch is a bit on the shallow side.

Under New Hampshire state law, it is illegal to deliberately harass water birds such as loons or ducks through the operation of a boat. Violators may be subject to fines and/or loss of their fishing license.

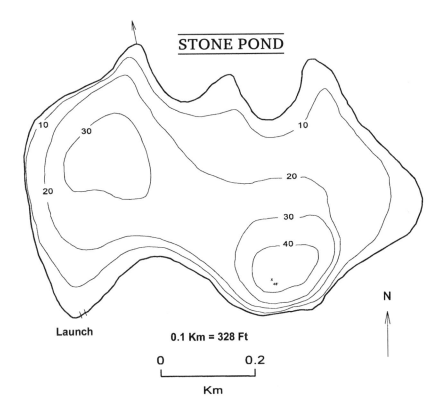

STONE POND

10   30

20

10

20

30

40

48"

Launch

0.1 Km = 328 Ft

0   0.2

Km

N

Lake Warren

ACRES: 185

MAX DEPTH: 14'   **MEAN DEPTH:** 7'

CLARITY: 12'   **ELEVATION:** 1200'

FISH SPECIES: Rainbow Trout, Brown Trout, Smallmouth Bass, Largemouth Bass, Pickerel, Horned Pout

ACCESS: Good ramp with parking for 4–6 vehicles.

DIRECTIONS: In Marlow, from the intersection of Routes 10 and 123, take Route 123 west 5.6 mi. The short access road is on your left. The access is just east of where the road passes close by the lake.

COMMENTS: A nice pond that supports a nice trout population as well as bass.

Bob houses used for ice fishing in winter must be removed from public waters, public property or private property prior to April 1 of each year. The owner's name and address are required by law to be plainly marked on the bob house.

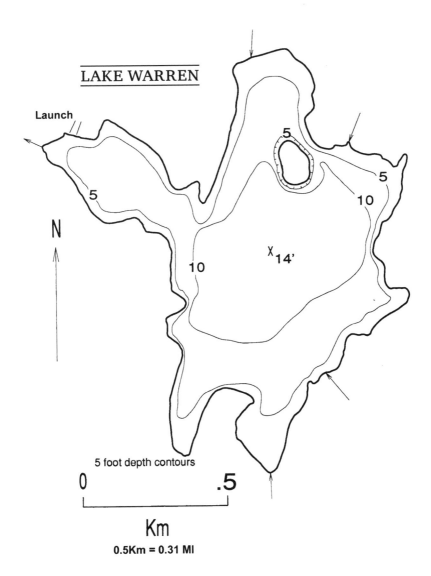

LAKE WARREN

Launch

5

5

5

10

10

N

X 14'

5 foot depth contours

0   .5

Km

0.5Km = 0.31 MI

Merrimack and Hillsboro Counties

Willard Pond in Antrim

Clough Pond

Loudon

ACRES: 46

MAX DEPTH: 57'   **MEAN DEPTH:** 16'

CLARITY: 14'   **ELEVATION:** 466'

FISH SPECIES: Brook Trout, Rainbow Trout

ACCESS: A nice ramp with parking for 4–5 vehicles.

DIRECTIONS: From the intersection of Routes 106 and 129 in Loudon, take Route 106 north 2.1 mi. to Clough Pond Road on the left. Go 1.2 mi. to the dam at Clough Pond. The access ramp is on the left.

COMMENTS: The boat ramp is adjacent to the town beach.

Take a close look at the structure of the shoreline and try to extend the elevation patterns into the lake. If you see a cliff, odds are the water is deep at its face. If you see a string of islands, odds are there is a shallow shoal that runs between them. Trout like drop-offs so you would want to troll parallel to the string of shoals and not over them.

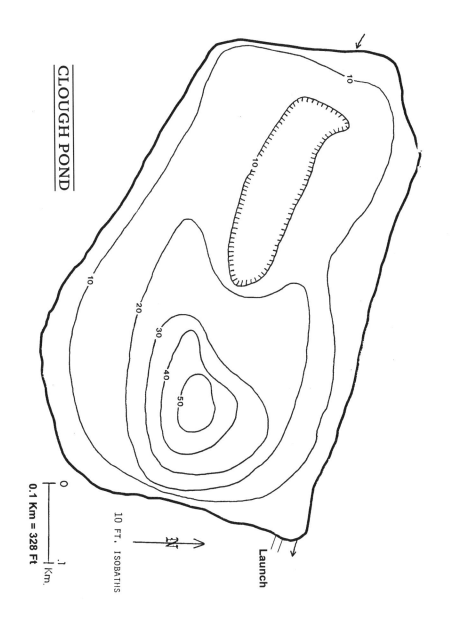

CLOUGH POND

10 FT. ISOBATHS

Launch

N

0.1 Km = 328 Ft

Highland Lake

ACRES: 211

MAX DEPTH: 44'   **MEAN DEPTH:** 16'

CLARITY: 19'   **ELEVATION:** 645'

FISH SPECIES: Brook Trout, Rainbow Trout, Smallmouth Bass

ACCESS: A nice paved ramp with good area to turn around. Parking is adequate for 5–6 vehicles.

DIRECTIONS: In East Andover (Halcyon Station), the ramp is right across the railroad tracks and opposite from the fire station on Route 11.

COMMENTS: This is a nice pond to fish. There is moderate development along the shoreline, and a healthy fish population.

> *An inexpensive and handy fishing reel cover
> is an old sock.*

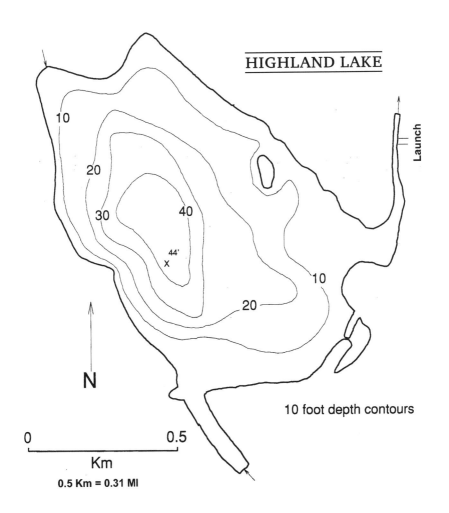

HIGHLAND LAKE

Launch

10

20

30

40

44'
X

10

20

N

10 foot depth contours

0   0.5
        Km
0.5 Km = 0.31 MI

Hot Hole Pond

Loudon

ACRES: 27

MAX DEPTH: 42'   **MEAN DEPTH:** 17'

CLARITY: 9'   **ELEVATION:** 481'

FISH SPECIES: Brook Trout, Rainbow Trout

ACCESS: A paved ramp and paved parking for 8–12 vehicles.

DIRECTIONS: From the intersection of Route 132 and Shaker Road in East Concord, follow Shaker Road north 3.0 mi. to Hot Hole Pond Road. Take a right and go 0.7 mi. to the boat ramp on the right.

COMMENTS: There is a handicap fishing access platform adjacent to the access ramp.

When in doubt about whether a fish you have caught is of legal size, it is always better to play it safe and release the fish unharmed back into the water.

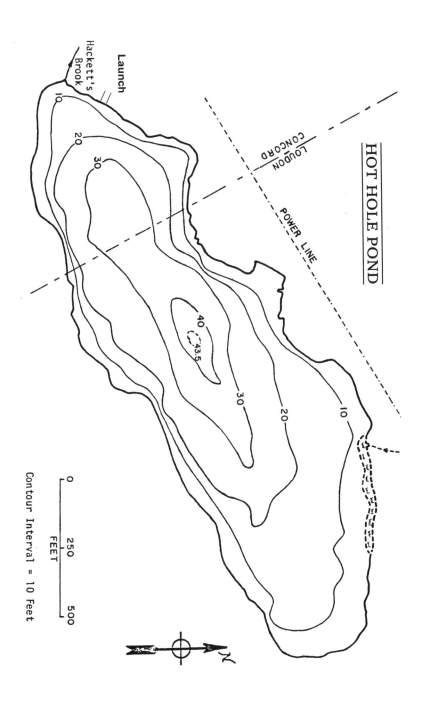

HOT HOLE POND

Hackett's Brook

Launch

LOUDON
CONCORD

POWER LINE

10

20

30

40

43.5

30

20

10

N

Contour Interval = 10 Feet

0   250   500
FEET

Hunts Pond

ACRES: 228

MAX DEPTH: 53' **MEAN DEPTH:** 15'

CLARITY: 22' **ELEVATION:** 1295'

FISH SPECIES: Brook Trout, Brown Trout, Smallmouth Bass, Largemouth Bass, Pickerel, Horned Pout

ACCESS: A dirt ramp with adequate parking for 4–6 vehicles.

DIRECTIONS: At the intersection of Routes 123 and 137 in Hancock, take Route 123 north for 2.3 mi. and turn left. (A sign also marks the road for the Harris Center.) Continue 0.6 mi. to a T intersection. The launch is to the right of the dam.

COMMENTS: This pond provides a good alternative to nearby Nubanusit Lake. Hunts Pond is fairly protected from the wind, too.

In order to remember the line test you have on a reel, write it on a small piece of tape stuck to the reel seat.

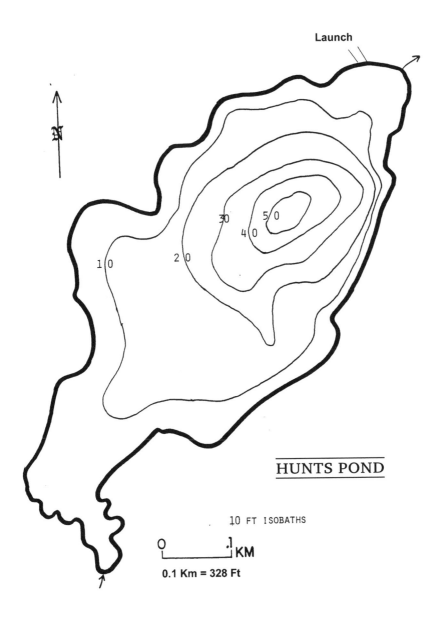

HUNTS POND

10 FT ISOBATHS

0.1 Km = 328 Ft

Kezar Lake

North Sutton

ACRES: 241

MAX DEPTH: 27'   **MEAN DEPTH:** 9'

CLARITY: 14'   **ELEVATION:** 906'

FISH SPECIES: Brook Trout, Rainbow Trout, Largemouth Bass, Smallmouth Bass, Pickerel, Horned Pout

ACCESS: A gravel ramp with parking for 8–10 vehicles.

DIRECTIONS: From North Sutton, follow signs to Wadleigh State Park (on Wadleigh Hill Road). After reaching the park, go 0.1 mi. and the launch is on your right.

COMMENTS: This is a nice pond bordered by a state park on its southeast shore.

If the fish you caught (and plan to release) is too exhausted to swim away, hold the fish upright in the water. Gently move the fish forward and backward so that the water runs through the gills. This is artificial resuscitation and may take a few minutes, especially in lakes. When the fish revives, begins to struggle and can swim normally, then release it.

SOURCE: NH FISH AND GAME

KEZAR LAKE

2 FT. ISOBATHS

N

PENACOOK ROAD

KEYSER STREET

WADLEIGH HILL ROAD

Launch

LOON

2 4 6 8 10 12 14 18 20 22

2 4 6 8 10 12 14

Little Sunapee Lake

New London

ACRES: 627

MAX DEPTH: 43' **MEAN DEPTH:** 14'

CLARITY: 16' **ELEVATION:** 1220'

FISH SPECIES: Rainbow Trout, Smallmouth Bass, Pickerel, Horned Pout

ACCESS: A gravel ramp next to the dam. Has adequate parking for 2–3 vehicles, with additional parking available on the road.

DIRECTIONS: From Exit 12 off I-89, go east on Route 114 (Newport Road) for 0.1 mi., then turn left. In just 0.1 mi., turn right onto Little Sunapee Road. The boat access is 0.25 mi. further on the right.

COMMENTS: Winds can be bothersome at times on this otherwise pleasant lake in the south-central part of the state.

Never remove a deeply swallowed hook from the fish's throat or stomach. If the hook is not easily removed, cut the leader and leave the hook in the fish. It will eventually work free or rust.

SOURCE: NH FISH AND GAME

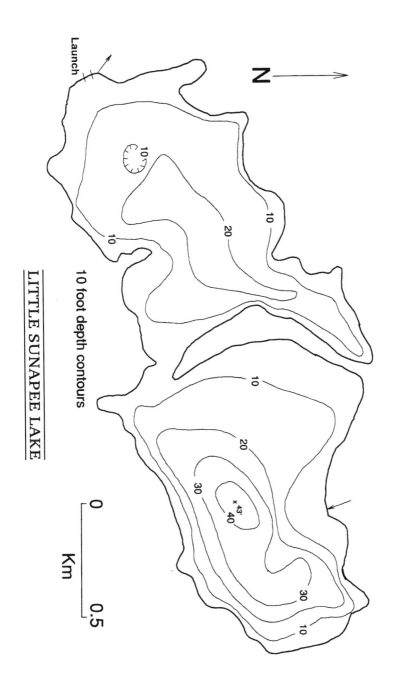

N

Launch

10 foot depth contours

LITTLE SUNAPEE LAKE

0   0.5
    Km

Mount William Pond

Weare

ACRES: 44

MAX DEPTH: 27'   **MEAN DEPTH:** 14'

CLARITY: 14'   **ELEVATION:** 830'

FISH SPECIES: Brown Trout, Rainbow Trout

ACCESS: A nice paved ramp with parking for 8–10 vehicles on the side of road.

DIRECTIONS: From the intersection of Routes 77 and 114 in South Weare, travel north 1.2 mi. to the top of a hill, where Mt. William Pond Road comes in on the right. Turn here and the ramp is straight ahead in just 200 feet.

COMMENTS: A nice quiet pond. Gas motors are not allowed.

The use of lead sinkers (1 ounce or less) and jigs (less than 1 inch along its longest axis) in freshwater lakes and ponds is prohibited in New Hampshire.

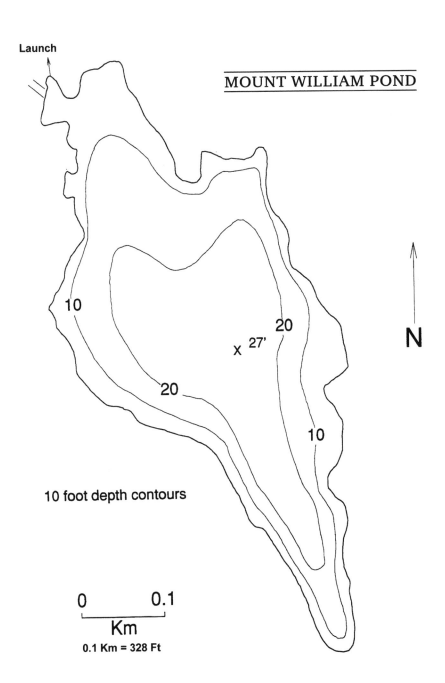

MOUNT WILLIAM POND

Launch

10

20

x 27'

20

10

10 foot depth contours

N

0   0.1
Km
0.1 Km = 328 Ft

Pleasant Lake

New London

ACRES: 606

MAX DEPTH: 94' **MEAN DEPTH:** 34'

CLARITY: 28' **ELEVATION:** 805'

FISH SPECIES: Brook Trout, Salmon, Pickerel, Horned Pout

ACCESS: A gravel launch. Parking is available across the road at the Masonic Lodge. Follow instructions on the signs.

DIRECTIONS: From Exit 11 off I-89, follow Route 11 east for 2.3 miles. Turn left onto Elkins Road. The boat access is 0.6 mi. on the left.

COMMENTS: The state record for Landlocked Salmon and Brook Trout were both taken from Pleasant Lake.

When fishing during the bug season, avoid using strong smelling soaps as it attracts the bugs.

PLEASANT LAKE

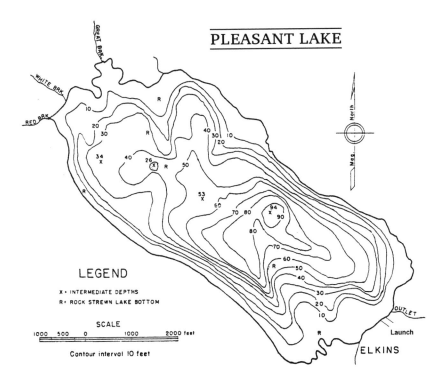

GREAT BRK

WHITE BRK

RED BRK

North

Mag.

R

10

20
30

40
30 10
20

34
X   40   26
X   R   50

R

53
X

50

70 80   94
X 90

80

70

60
R 50
40

30

20
10
OUTLET

R   Launch

ELKINS

LEGEND

X = INTERMEDIATE DEPTHS
R = ROCK STREWN LAKE BOTTOM

SCALE

1000 500 0   1000   2000 feet

Contour interval 10 feet

Waukeena Lake (a/k/a Pleasant Pond)

Danbury

ACRES: 53

MAX DEPTH: 20' **MEAN DEPTH:** 6'

CLARITY: 6' **ELEVATION:** 1116'

FISH SPECIES: Rainbow Trout, Brook Trout

ACCESS: A gravel ramp with parking for 4–5 vehicles.

DIRECTIONS: From Route 4 in the center of Danbury, cross over the railroad tracks and proceed 0.2 mi. before turning right onto High Street. Follow this road for 0.3 miles and turn left onto Waukeena Lake Road. Continue 1.5 mi. to ramp on the right.

COMMENTS: Although it looks like a Bass pond, it is stocked with Brook and Rainbow Trout. It's a nice quiet pond with plenty of birds and wildlife to keep you entertained. There are no gas motors allowed.

> *Tiger Trout are a cross between the Brook Trout and the Brown Trout.*

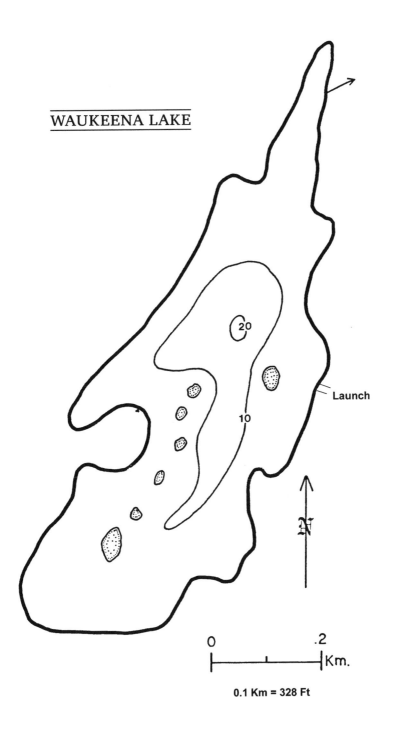

WAUKEENA LAKE

Launch

20

10

N

0   .2

Km.

0.1 Km = 328 Ft

Webster Lake

Franklin

ACRES: 813

MAX DEPTH: 39' **MEAN DEPTH:** 18'

CLARITY: 16' **ELEVATION:** 401'

FISH SPECIES: Rainbow Trout, Brown Trout, Smallmouth Bass, Largemouth Bass, Pickerel, Horned Pout

ACCESS: A paved ramp with parking for 10–15 vehicles. The launch is next to the town beach.

DIRECTIONS: From the intersection of Routes 11 and 3A in Franklin, follow Route 11 west 1.0 mi. The launch is on the right.

COMMENTS: This is a popular lake during the summer months, but still provides good fishing.

Check the drag on your reel each time you tie a new lure on. Many fish have been lost to an improperly set drag.

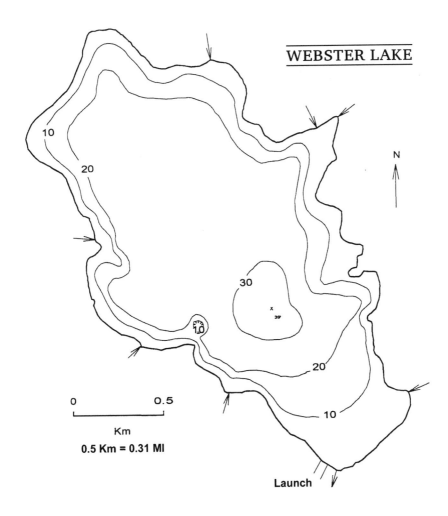

WEBSTER LAKE

N

10

20

30

X
39

10

20

10

0   0.5

Km

0.5 Km = 0.31 MI

Launch

Whittemore Lake

Bennington

ACRES: 55

MAX DEPTH: 50' **MEAN DEPTH:** 27'

CLARITY: 18' **ELEVATION:** 828'

FISH SPECIES: Brook Trout, Brown Trout, Rainbow Trout

ACCESS: A dirt ramp with adequate parking for 8–10 vehicles.

DIRECTIONS: From the center of Bennington, take Route 31 south for 1.7 mi. The access road is on the right.

COMMENTS: The boat ramp is adjacent to the town beach. No motorboats or boats equipped with an outboard motor are allowed.

> *Brown Trout are native to Western Europe and were first formally stocked in the U.S. on April 11, 1884, in Michigan's Pere Marquette River.*

WHITTEMORE LAKE

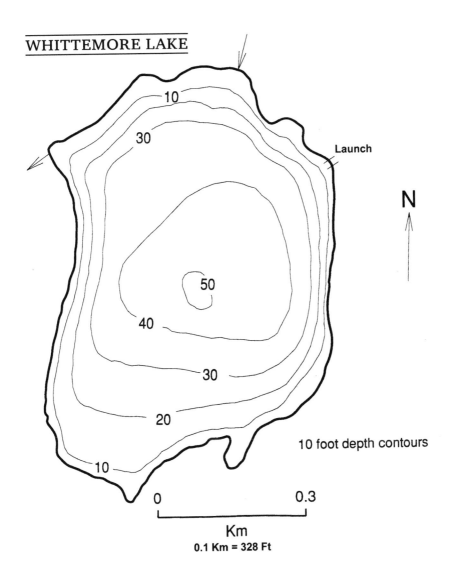

Launch

10

30

50

40

30

20

10

10 foot depth contours

N

0   0.3

Km

0.1 Km = 328 Ft

Willard Pond

Antrim

ACRES: 97

MAX DEPTH: 65' **MEAN DEPTH:** 26'

CLARITY: 32' **ELEVATION:** 1158'

FISH SPECIES: Brook Trout, Rainbow Trout, Tiger Trout

ACCESS: A dirt ramp. A parking area large enough for 10–15 vehicles is located a short walk away from the launch.

DIRECTIONS: From the intersection of Routes 9 and 123 in South Stoddard, follow Route 123 south toward Hancock. In 3.4 mi., turn left onto Willard Pond Road. Staying left at a subsequent fork, it is 1.7 mi. to the pond.

COMMENTS: This is a *Fly Fishing Only* pond. No gas motors are allowed, either. The pond is located in an Audubon Society Refuge. It is stocked with Tiger, Brook and Rainbow Trout.

Be aware of your shadow. If you cast your shadow across a fish, it will flee to the nearest hiding place.

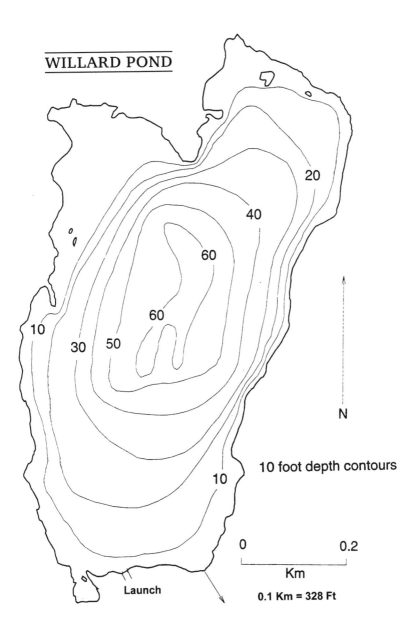

WILLARD POND

20

40

60

60

10

30 50

10

N

10 foot depth contours

0   0.2

Km

0.1 Km = 328 Ft

Launch

Belknap, Rockingham and Strafford Counties

Massabesic Lake in Auburn

Beaver Lake

Derry

ACRES: 134

MAX DEPTH: 45'   **MEAN DEPTH:** 16'

CLARITY: 11'   **ELEVATION:** 290'

FISH SPECIES: Brook Trout, Rainbow Trout, Smallmouth Bass, Largemouth Bass, Pickerel, Horned Pout, Blue Gill

ACCESS: A paved ramp with a nice turnaround. There is parking for 10 vehicles with trailers.

DIRECTIONS: From the intersection of the Route 28 Bypass and Route 102 in Derry Village, take Route 102 north 1.0 mi. to Pond Road on right. Turn here and go 0.25 mi. to the launch on the right.

COMMENTS: The ramp is nice enough, but parking is way under the demand. Beaver Lake is a nice two-tier fishery.

Mark your boat paddle or oar to indicate inches and you'll have a handy scale to measure your catch.

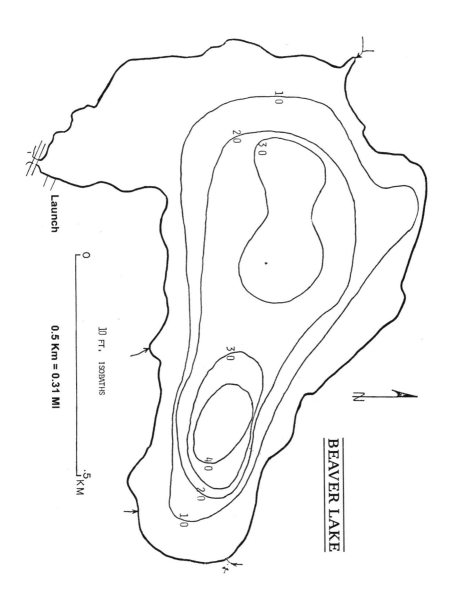

Launch

0   .5 KM

10 FT. ISOBATHS

0.5 Km = 0.31 MI

N

BEAVER LAKE

Bow Lake

Strafford

ACRES: 1161

MAX DEPTH: 69'   **MEAN DEPTH:** 21'

CLARITY: 22'   **ELEVATION:** 1690'

FISH SPECIES: Rainbow Trout, Brown Trout, Largemouth Bass, Smallmouth Bass, Pickerel, Horned Pout, White Perch

ACCESS: A nice paved ramp off the side of the road.

DIRECTIONS: From the center or Northwood where Routes 4, 9, and 202 meet, take Routes 202 & 9 north 0.3 mi. to the intersection with Route 202A on the left. Take 202A 3.2 mi. to Province Road, then take a left and go 0.1 mi. to Water Street (on left). Note that parking is here, by the dam. Continue another 0.2 mi. to the ramp.

COMMENTS: Please note that parking for the boat ramp is at a different location from the ramp. Parking near the dam is adequate for 10–15 vehicles. There is a state dock located closer to the parking, so that the person in the boat can pick up the one parking the car. It's a two-person operation!

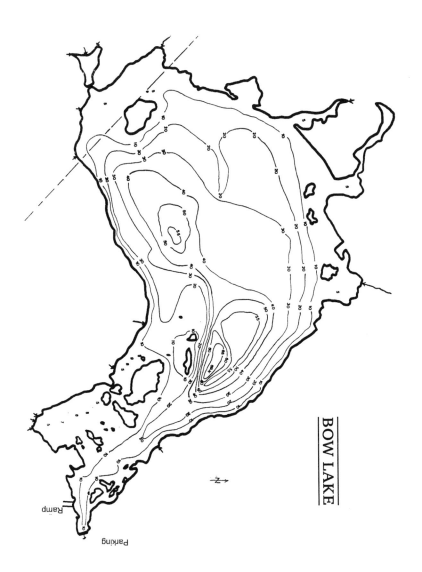

BOW LAKE

Manning Lake

ACRES: 202

MAX DEPTH: 54'   **MEAN DEPTH:** 20'

CLARITY: 20'   **ELEVATION:** 715'

FISH SPECIES: Brook Trout, Largemouth Bass, Smallmouth Bass, Pickerel, Horned Pout

ACCESS: A paved ramp with parking for 5–8 vehicles.

DIRECTIONS: From Gilmanton Ironworks, take Route 140 west 0.3 mi. to Crystal Lake Road on the right. Take Crystal Lake Road past its namesake lake and at 3.0 mi. go left onto Guinea Ridge Road. Follow this road 1.9 mi. to access road on the right. Continue 0.5 mi. to the launch.

COMMENTS: Although Manning Lake is classified as a warm water lake, it is stocked with Brook Trout.

Please only keep what you eat, and resolve to eat what you have damaged.

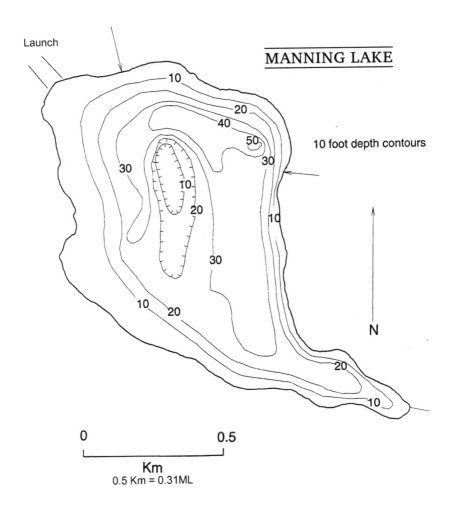

Launch

MANNING LAKE

10 foot depth contours

N

0   0.5

Km
0.5 Km = 0.31ML

Massabesic Lake

Auburn

ACRES: 2512

MAX DEPTH: 60'   **MEAN DEPTH:** 17'

CLARITY: 15'   **ELEVATION:** 249'

FISH SPECIES: Brook Trout, Rainbow Trout, Brown Trout, Smallmouth Bass, Largemouth Bass, Pickerel, Horned Pout, White Perch, Northern Pike, Black Crappie

ACCESS: A nice wide, gravel ramp with parking for 15–20 vehicles.

DIRECTIONS: From the center of Auburn, follow Route 121 south 0.5 mi. The access ramp area is on the right.

COMMENTS: Massabesic Lake is the water supply for the City of Manchester. There is no swimming or wading allowed.

Landlocked Salmon usually bite better on cloudy, windy days than when the skies are sunny.

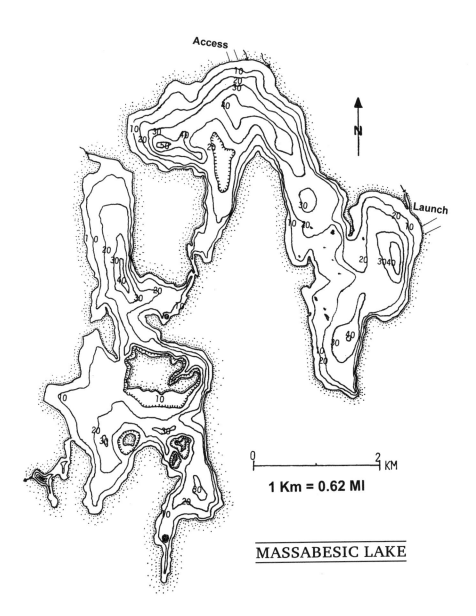

Access

N

Launch

0   2
KM

1 Km = 0.62 MI

MASSABESIC LAKE

Merrymeeting Lake

New Durham

ACRES: IIII

MAX DEPTH: 135' **MEAN DEPTH:** 49'

CLARITY: 34' **ELEVATION:** 639'

FISH SPECIES: Rainbow Trout, Salmon, Lake Trout, Smallmouth Bass, Pickerel, Horned Pout

ACCESS: A good gravel ramp near the dam. Parking is available for 10–14 vehicles.

DIRECTIONS: At the intersection of Routes 11 and 28 in Alton, take Route 11 east 3.0 mi., then turn left onto Depot Road. At 0.3 mi., turn left, then go 0.6 mi. and turn right. Continue another 3.0 mi., then stay left at an intersection. The boat access is on the right, near the dam.

COMMENTS: This is a nice lake to troll during the spring fishing season.

> *Brook and Brown Trout spawn in the fall;*
> *Rainbow Trout spawn in the spring.*

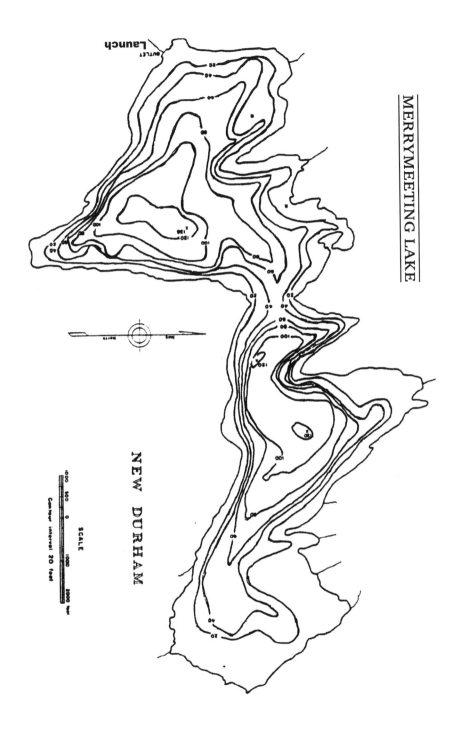

MERRYMEETING LAKE

NEW DURHAM

Launch

SCALE

Contour interval 20 feet

Opechee Bay

Laconia

ACRES: 427

MAX DEPTH: 57'   **MEAN DEPTH:** 25'

CLARITY: 26'   **ELEVATION:** 492'

FISH SPECIES: Rainbow Trout, Largemouth Bass, Small-mouth Bass, Pickerel, Horned Pout, White Perch

ACCESS: A paved ramp with parking for 10–15 vehicles.

DIRECTIONS: From Route 106 North (Main Street) in downtown Laconia, turn right onto Church Street. Take first left onto Messer Street and continue 0.6 mi. After crossing over bridge, look for access ramp on the left next to electric power transfer station.

COMMENTS: This facility is open to the public courtesy of Public Service of New Hampshire and the City of Laconia. This is primarily a warm water fishery. It is, however, stocked with Rainbow Trout.

> *Trout depend mostly on sight to locate food.*

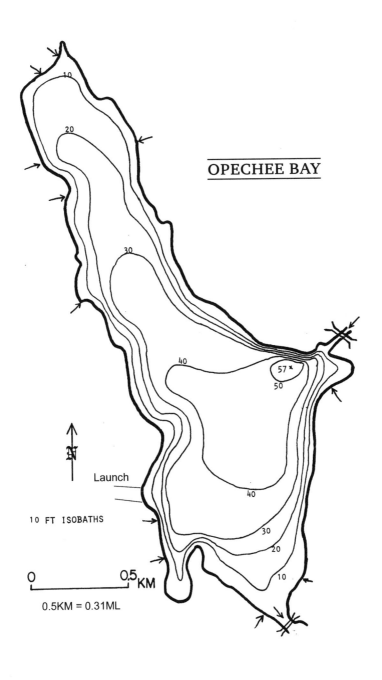

OPECHEE BAY

10

20

30

40

57 ×

50

N

Launch

10 FT ISOBATHS

40

30

20

10

0   0.5 KM

0.5KM = 0.31ML

Lake Waukewan

Meredith

ACRES: 913

MAX DEPTH: 70' **MEAN DEPTH:** 22'

CLARITY: 20' **ELEVATION:** 539'

FISH SPECIES: Rainbow Trout, Smallmouth Bass, Pickerel, Horned Pout

ACCESS: A gravel ramp with parking for 10–15 vehicles.

DIRECTIONS: From the intersection of Routes 3 and 25 in Meredith, head south for 0.4 mi. and turn right onto Waukewan Street. Continue 0.4 mi. to boat access on right.

COMMENTS: The daily limit for Brook, Rainbow or Brown Trout on Lake Waukewan is two fish. No gas-powered motors are allowed on the lake.

Avoid contact with your lures or bait after putting on insect repellant or sunscreen.

LAKE WAUKEWAN

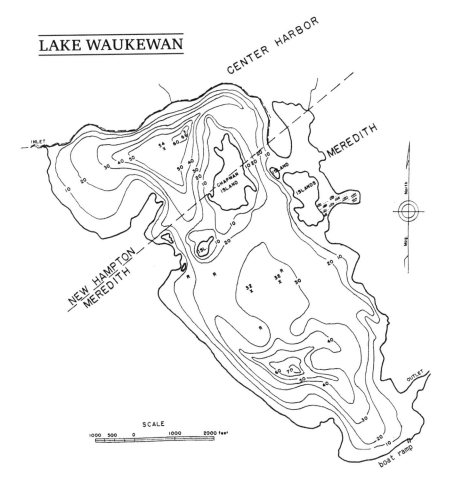

Index